The D.I. Guide to Residential Integration

Todd B. Adams

The D.I. Guide to Residential Integration

Published by

www.dipartner.com

Copyright 2003, 2004 by dipartner.com

All source files for this book may be found at **www.dipartner. com** for registered owners of this book. Upon registration, you will be granted access to a special download area of the site to retrieve updated information pertaining to this book, for a period of one year.

Library of Congress Cataloging-in-Publication Data:

Library of Congress Control Number: 2004110926

ISBN: 0-9760562-0-8

Manufactured in the United States of America

About this book

This book and its companion download are intended to be used as a resource and a reference tool. The material includes technical information and blank templates. The book and downloads represent thousands of hours of "hands-on" experience in the Home Integration industry. Both provide the information and tools you can use to bring your company into the field of total home integration.

The topics covered in this book are: music systems, lighting, HVAC, security, user interfaces, central control system, and structured wiring. This book contains a brief section on home theatres, but does not contain in-depth information on them. That information will be available in another book.

We have worked, as you do, in the day-to-day struggle of keeping a company viable and growing. We know the difficulties you face every day. Our book and downloads can help eliminate some of your growing pains by providing you with technical information and templates so you can accurately meet your customer's expectations.

We have left blank pages for notes at the end of each section for your use. Also in complex installation sections, we have left space for notes in a column on the right side of the page.

Please remember the material in this book and its companion download are copyrighted.

You must request our express written permission to copy or modify this material for your use or your company's use. However, you are free to use the blank templates in the download to prepare your proposals to your customers. If you have any questions regarding the material in this book, or want to request permission to copy any portion of it, please contact us at

www.dipartner.com

About the Author

Todd B. Adams

Todd Adams is founder and CEO of DIpartner.com. He has 10 years of experience in home integration design, engineering, installation, and sales. He has an in–depth understanding of networking and network administration.

Founder and CEO at Cutting Edge Systems Corporation, a company focusing on home integration systems in high–end homes throughout New England, Todd established procedures for maintaining operations, product quality, reliability, installation and safety. He provided strategic planning, researched new products, and implemented vendor partnerships. He managed all proposal development.

He has written articles for industry magazines and has been quoted in industry publications, including "Residential Systems," "Custom Installer," and "CE Pro," as well as in "The Boston Globe". During his tenure, Cutting Edge Systems Corporation was well respected in the industry, won many industry awards and was featured in "The Robb Report" and "Audio Video Interiors". He has taught at numerous industry conferences.

At CEDIA (Custom Design and Installation Association) in 2002, he received the CEDIA Design I Certification, CEDIA Lifestyle award for Home Theater of the Year, and Volunteer of the Year for his work on the education council. He began his career in the mid–80s at Raytheon Equipment Corporation, as a design and test engineer on the Stinger, AAMRAM, and Patriot Missile projects.

In 2003, Todd decided to move in a new direction and established DIpartner.com, a national template and web site organization dedicated to helping home theater companies grow and move into the field of home integration.

Acknowledgements

Without the enncouragement, advise, and thoughtful review of those mentioned below this book would not be possible. Thank you for all of your hard work and incredible insight.

Book Reviewers

Chappel Cory – Multimedia Technologies

Ken Erdmann – The Edrmann Group

Gerry Demple – Ulitmate Electronics

Gordan van Zuiden – Cybermanor

John Gerhart – Lutron Electronics

Ken Smith – Custom Electronics

John White – Russound

Editor

Maggie Adams

Technical Drawings

Ryan Morton

Cover Design

Stephen Fernandez

Contents

BEFORE THE PROJECT STARTS

STRUCTURED WIRING

KEYPADS & TOUCHSCREENS

MUSIC INTEGRATION

LIGHTING INTEGRATION

HVAC INTEGRATION

SECURITY INTEGRATION

THEATER INTEGRATION

GLOSSARY

I

INTRODUCTION

Chapter One

How to use this book

I find that a great part of the information I have, was acquired by looking up something and finding something else on the way.

– Franklin Pierce Adams (1881–1960) American columnist & author

We have designed this book so that it can be used as a reference and resource by those in home integration companies that are just starting out, are more established, or already are advanced in custom installation services. No matter where your company is in its growth process, you can use this book. Here's how each level can take advantage of the extensive material presented.

Beginning Residential Integration Company – For the novice company, the book is designed so that you can use the material exactly as presented. Each piece – customer proposals, installation instructions, and project management – provides the basic information to work on a project from start to finish. We've even included the letters to send to subcontractors requesting their assistance in installing various systems that will tie into your integration system. Each piece has been designed to fit together in a logical, cohesive manner.

Intermediate Residential Integration Company – As a more established company, we understand you already may have developed relationships with certain products and manufacturers. Continue to use those vendors by substituting their products for those suggested in this book. Think of the book as a guide or flexible plan you can follow. Stick with the book's core ideas, and adapt them to your specific products. Stay within the scope of the design philosophy described in this book.

Advanced Residential Integration Company – As an established company, we challenge you to start to develop your company's own philosophy, and establish your own values toward your company's customers. Use the processes described in this book as a skeletal plan to help you develop your own standards.

How to get the download?

The download portion of this book includes the following;

The Sample Project – This will include every document discussed in this book and a few more completely filled out for our sample client. We also include a set of floor plans to review to see how these documents actually apply to the home.

Templates – For each document discussed in this book we provide easy–to–alter templates in Microsoft Word. We have included a few extras to help you get organized.

To get the download go to **www.dipartner.com**. Select the "Register" button right on the top page. It will take you through the process of setting up your account on **www.dipartner.com**. In addition to requesting a few things about you and your company, you will be asked for your registration number, which can be found at the back of this book.

The information in the download will be kept up to date and you will be notified via e–mail when new downloads are available. This will ensure you have the latest information.

Job Descriptions

Why are job descriptions important? Job descriptions clarify the responsibilities for the position, list qualifications desired, enable performance evaluations, show the relationship of a position to other positions in the company, and provide a basis for salary and salary increases. Job descriptions can also help you determine which jobs may be eliminated in lean times, or which ones can be temporary.

We have listed below brief descriptions of various positions that are generally needed in residential custom installation companies. Depending on the size of your company, you may have one person performing the role of two or more positions. Or you may have one or more persons filling each role.

Throughout this book we will be referring to the following job descriptions.

Sales Representative

Initiates sales leads, develops long–term customer relationships, sells company products and services, follows through projects from start to finish to ensure customer satisfaction. Networks with residential builders, interior designers, architects, and homeowners to develop optimum sales potential and future customers. This position requires a thorough understanding of the residential building industry. Assists in developing pricing strategy.

Requires a college degree and at least five to seven years of experience in sales.

Project Manager

Plans and directs the project flow from start to finish, provides guidance to installers and subcontractors throughout the project, develops relationships with and coordinates all communication with builders, architects, interior designers, contractors and customers.

Initiates contact with the customer at the start of the project, conducts site reviews and initial consultation with the sales representative to gain a thorough understanding of the scope of the project. Prepares documentation throughout the project.

Requires a solid understanding of the residential integration process, design and installation of music systems, lighting, telephone, HVAC, and security. Must have a thorough understanding of millwork design, construction standards, low–voltage cabling practices, and safety code regulations. Position requires a comprehensive understanding of construction documentation (plans, elevations, sections) and be able to coordinate detailed projects through completion.

Requires a college degree and at least five to seven years of experience in managing construction projects.

Software Engineer

Plans, documents, and maintains all aspects of system programming to include user interface (keypads and touchscreens) designs, infrared files, and programming files. Develops and maintains archives of all customer programming and documentation when the project is closed. Ensures that all programming is completed and tested in advance of the installation date. Supervises and works closely with in–house technicians to ensure that every system installed in the customer's home is built correctly and fully functional. Prepares user manuals for the customer. Also provides training for technicians to develop their software skills.

Requires Bachelor of Science degree in computer science and two years experience.

Hardware Design Engineer

Plans, designs and develops hardware solutions for custom installation projects. Works closely with the project manager and other engineers to move projects forward. Applies principles of engineering, science and mathematics to resolve hardware design problems. Researches third–party products to integrate into solutions to meet customer needs.

Requires Bachelor of Science degree in engineering or computer science and two years professional experience.

Mechanical Engineer

Plans, designs and creates detailed architectural solutions for residential installations using 2D CAD software. Provides technical support, installation instructions, and equipment specifications to the installation team. Determines potential hardware conflicts, sizing, ventilation, and structural support issues within the project. Communicates, as necessary, with builders, architects, electricians, cabinet-makers and other tradesmen on the job.

Requires Bachelor of Science degree in mechanical engineering and at least three years professional experience.

Lighting Engineer

Designs, documents, programs, manages and services lighting control systems. Applies engineering, science and mathematics principles in solving design issues. Works with and provides appropriate instruction to electricians, lighting designers, interior designers, architects, and subcontractors associated with the lighting control system. Notifies Project Manager of any system changes that need to be written into a revised contract. Assists in customer training when project finishes. Follows up and coordinates "final" lighting adjustments. Visits the site after the customer has moved into the home.

Requires a college degree and at least three years experience.

Technicians versus Installers

We have included three positions that are classified as technician and two that are classified as installer.

Technicians work on the electronic aspects of the projects. Their role is to perform tasks, such as build the equipment rack, make final connections and troubleshoot the systems. Technicians will use more advanced test equipment such as audio and video analyzers. Typically a technician has some education beyond high school, usually a two-year technical school.

Installers work on the trade portion of the project. Installers carry the project from cabling to the move-in phase. They use power tools, such as drills and saws, to work with the structure of the home. In addition installers will test the cabling using a variety of testing tools. Installers typically have a vocational background, and follow the traditional apprentice/master training path.

Lead Technician

Knows and understands the in-house and field technician roles. Provides guidance and directs activities of team members. Oversees team schedule on a week-to-week basis to meet priorities outlined by the Project Manager. Estimates labor hour requirements for completion of project. Interprets company standards and enforces safety regulations. Monitors performance of team and suggests changes for improved efficiency. Analyzes and resolves technical work problems, and assists team members in solving technical work problems.

Some education beyond two-year technical school is highly desirable. Two years experience of in-house and field technician roles is required.

In-House Technician

Uses appropriate drawings and documentation to verify and test systems and their components prior to programming and delivery to the customer. Assembles equipment racks. Tests all active components that plug into an AC outlet for functionality. Prepares keypads and touchscreens for programming. Organizes user manuals and small parts that come with the equipment in a project file box for the customer. Coordinates with the software engineer to schedule programming the system. Works closely with purchasing to order required rack parts/components based on bill of materials, drawings and documentation.

Two-year technical school degree and one year experience, or four years of practical experience.

Field Technician

Delivers the equipment rack to the project site during the equipment installation phase, and connects cables at distribution panels to the equipment rack. Installs keypads and touchscreens throughout the home. Uses cable testing equipment to troubleshoot problems. Has a clear understanding of the purpose and function of distribution panels and the connections to the integrated system. Installs system telephones and makes connections to the telephone system and tests programming for customer preferences. Assists in customer education/training, when requested.

Two-year technical school degree plus one year experience, or four years of practical experience in electronics.

Lead Installer

Knows and understands the installer role. Provides guidance and directs activities of team members. Oversees team schedule on a week-to-week basis to meet priorities outlined by the Project Manager. Estimates labor hour requirements for completion of project. Interprets company standards and enforces safety regulations. Monitors performance of team and suggests changes for improved efficiency. Analyzes and resolves technical work problems, and assists team members in solving technical work problems.

Some education beyond two-year technical school is highly desirable. Two years experience of in-house and field technician roles is required.

Installer

Pulls cables, such as coaxial, category 5e, audio, twisted pair, and other cable types, between walls, above ceilings and between floors in residential structures. Installs open conduit to link all areas of the home for future accessibility. Uses cable testing equipment to troubleshoot problems. Handles basic cable dressing (i.e. final trim lengths and labeling). Installs modular connectors and wallplates for data, telephone, audio, television, and other low-voltage applications. Terminates cable on cross connects, hubs, and routers in accordance with structured wiring standards using proper cable connector tools, approved connector installation techniques and correct connector pin-out standards. Installs and mounts interface devices, control devices, structural/mechanical devices, architectural devices, and display devices. Observes safety practices and procedures (including ongoing job site maintenance and cleanliness practices and procedures).

Requires a high school degree or a GED.

Phases of the Project

Sales Process

For the purpose of this book, we will only summarize the sales process. We plan to explore the process in depth in a future book. The sales process encompasses a number of key functions before the project, throughout the project, and after the project is completed. The sales person generates leads, qualifies the leads, generates proposals and closes the deal. Throughout the project, the sales person works with engineering to ensure that company standards are being met, and, at the same time, balances the needs of the customer.

The sales person works closely with the engineering group to develop the customer proposal. The sales person is responsible for listening to the customer to determine what the customer wants. The engineering group takes that information and puts it in a formal proposal to the customer. The sales person presents the customer proposal, explains it, and negotiates changes requested by the customer. We have provided templates for customer proposals in this book that can be filled in, altered, or modified to fit your customer's choices.

The sales person also gathers the customer's specific preferences, such as color of wallplates, temperature setpoints and keypad locations. We have included "Customer Information" sheets to assist in gathering this information. We recommend that the sales person assist the customer in filling out these sheets. Engineering and sales then use the final customer proposal, which defines the project requirements, and the information sheets, which list the specific number of keypads, touchscreens, thermostats and other system details, to develop the company's pricing strategy for that project.

When the project is closed, the sales person continues to maintain a relationship with the customer for possible future sales and service.

22

Project Open

The project open starts only after the customer has signed the contract and handed over the initial payment for the project. Make sure that you allow adequate time to perform all of the functions in this phase. In other words, don't take the check on Tuesday and promise the customer you'll be there on Wednesday to start the cabling.

We have devoted a chapter in this book to describing this most important phase. Opening the project includes ordering consumer electronics, system components, a variety of electronic parts, notifying related trades, placing stickers in the home designating the locations for wallplates, keypads, touchscreens and thermostats, and creating extensive project folders for each team – sales, project management, installation, and engineering teams.

Cabling

This phase is explained in detail in the chapter, "Structured Wiring". The bulk of this phase involves installing the cables throughout the home. This makes sense since it's called the cabling phase!

Termination

The termination phase is covered in depth in the chapter, "Structured Wiring". This phase is when you terminate, test, and label all of the cables throughout the home.

Move–In

This phase also is explained in depth in the chapter, "Structured Wiring". During the last few days of construction, the move–in crew attaches wallplates, installs speakers, makes active connections for telephone and television, and prepares the home for a certificate of occupancy (CO).

In order to get a CO, the low–voltage cabling must pass an inspection, generally conducted by the electrical inspector. Other work on the home, such as HVAC, plumbing and electrical wiring also must pass inspection. When all of the categories of work pass the building inspection, a CO is issued and the owner may move in.

To simplify the inspection process, and cut down on the possibility of failing inspection, it is best to delay installing the electronics until after the inspection process is completed. Your goal during this phase is for the customer to move into his/her new home. To do that it is not necessary to connect the HVAC systems, the lighting system, or the music system to the house–wide integration system. Those connections are not required to receive a CO. Once the CO is issued, the touchscreens can be installed, the music system can be brought in and installed, the security and HVAC systems can be connected to the main integration system. Some customers prefer waiting to move into their new home until all these systems are in place, even though they could move in earlier. The electronics are not necessary to live in the house, or receive the formal CO.

Plan on making the final connections to HVAC and security systems after each of their respective subcontractors are through the tinkering process and the customer is happy with each system. This may be up to a month after the customer has moved in. Do not integrate any subsystem until that system has been thoroughly tested and used by the customer.

Programming & Building Equipment

Some phases are conducted off site at your company's office. In this phase, the engineering group takes all of the customer preferences from the "Customer Information" sheets and uses it to program the standard modules to these preferences. The equipment is purchased and installed into equipment racks, and tested with all of the keypads and touchscreens. Very important: do not deliver any system that has not gone through this process or has not been thoroughly tested. It is better to deliver a working system late than an incomplete, untested system on time.

Electronics

The chapters, "Keypads and Touchscreens", "Music Systems", and "Home Theatre", describe and define the processes of this phase. The electronics team delivers the equipment rack, connects cables to the distribution panels, and installs keypads and touchscreens.

Training

When the system is designed and installed properly, very little training will be needed. Do not allow the customer to use the system until the system installation is completed. It is best to unplug it at the end of every day during the installation period. Set up a mutual time for training and demonstrating the system to the customer and notify him/her that the final payment is due at that time. It is best to gather the family for training, make the event special and bring a gift that is appropriate for the level system purchased. Explain the service policy at that time. Even though training may seem simple to you, it may take the customer some time to adjust to a new way of doing things. Be prepared to be patient and answer customer questions. The new integrated system provides convenience, comfort, and an enhanced lifestyle to your customer, but it probably will mean a brief period of adjustment for the family.

Service

You must establish a service period with appropriate charges in order to both be profitable and provide continued service for your customer. Figure 1.1 is a suggested guide to establishing service rates. The table represents charges based on a percentage of the total project cost. CEDIA has an excellent program for underwriting the costs of these service periods. In addition to those charges absorbed by the underwritten program add in your own services, like semi–annual maintenance, to tailor the service package to your customers.

If the customer is currently not in one of these plans you must establish hourly service rates, including minimum charges and travel charges.

Service Period	Charge
90 days	Free
1 year	3%
3 years	8%
5 years	13%

Figure 1.1
Service Charges

Staff Involvement in the Project

Phase	Sales Person	Project Manager	Install-ers	Techni-cians	Engi-neers
Sales	X				X
Project Open	X	X			X
Cabling	X	X	X		
Termination		X	X		
Programming & Build	X	X		X	X
Move–In		X	X		
Electronics		X		X	X
Training		X			X

Figure 1.2
Staffing by phase

Beginning Company

Figure 1.3
Beginning
Org Chart

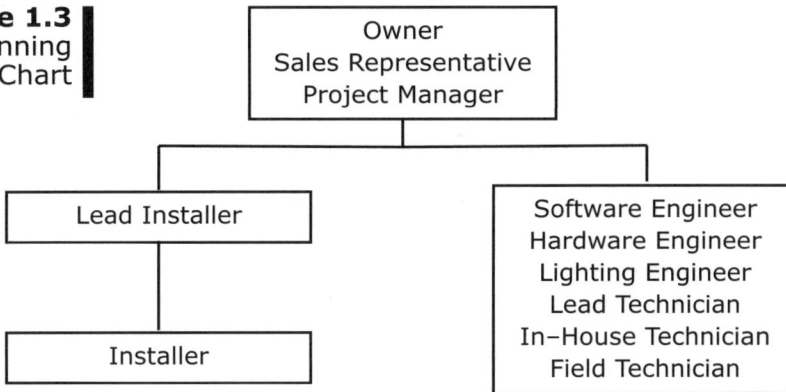

```
                    ┌─────────────────────────┐
                    │          Owner          │
                    │   Sales Representative   │
                    │     Project Manager      │
                    └─────────────────────────┘
           ┌────────────────┴──────────────────┐
   ┌───────────────────┐          ┌─────────────────────────┐
   │   Lead Installer   │          │    Software Engineer    │
   └───────────────────┘          │    Hardware Engineer    │
           │                      │    Lighting Engineer    │
   ┌───────────────────┐          │     Lead Technician     │
   │     Installer      │          │    In–House Technician  │
   └───────────────────┘          │     Field Technician    │
                                  └─────────────────────────┘
```

In figure 1.3 we show a four–person company. The owner is also the project manager and the sales represenatative. He/She has three employees, each of which is technical and focused on getting the work done. This scenario works well for a company with less than roughly $500K per year in revenues.

Keep in mind that the company will grow and standards are important if you wish to grow the company beyond this point. Imagine hiring someone into the company to service your installed projects. Although you are starting out as a small company a strong foundatioin is required to grow to the next level. Build that foundation at this time!

You're off to a great start! Stick to the systems we have laid out in this book and start to think about your customers as a demographic. What things do all of your customers have in common? How can you leverage the things you learn from one customer across all of your future customers?

You'll be ready for the next business model before you know it.

Intermediate Company

Figure 1.4
Intermediate
Org Chart

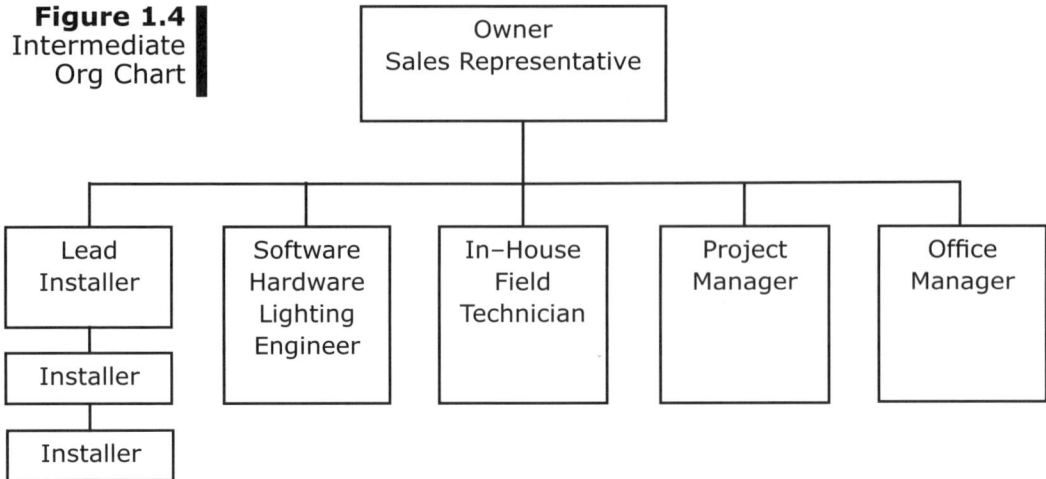

```
                        ┌─────────────────────┐
                        │        Owner         │
                        │  Sales Representative │
                        └─────────────────────┘
```

| Lead Installer | Software Hardware Lighting Engineer | In-House Field Technician | Project Manager | Office Manager |

Installer

Installer

In figure 1.4 we show an eight-person company. The owner still is the sales representative and drives the entire customer interface in the company. The employees start to take on a more focused approach. This scenario works well for a company with less than roughly $1 million per year in revenues.

The owner at this point should start to develop ways to decrease customer interaction. Think about bringing in someone to handle customers after the system is complete. Assign to your technician perform the customer training and handle the customer's service issues. Think about bringing in a person, who generates leads, gives architect presentations, visit builders, and sends out information to prospective leads.

You have done well through the first stage of growth. Prepare for the next stage by documenting company standards, having regular meetings with the executive team to focus on building the company.

Advanced Company

Figure 1.5 Advanced Org Chart

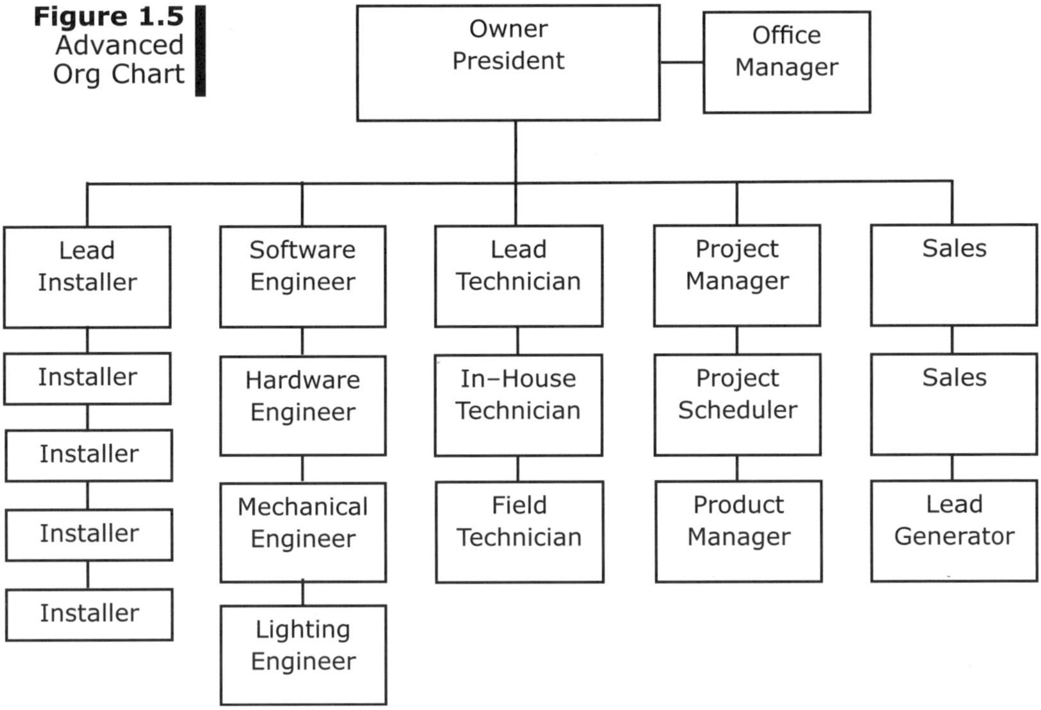

In figure 1.5 we show a 20-person company. The owner has separated from the day-to-day installation and customer interaction process. Instead, the owner assumes a more formal operations role. The employees are very focused on specific tasks and work well as a team. This scenario works well for a company with less than roughly $5 million per year in revenues.

There are still many challenges that face this size company. How will you compete with smaller companies who do not share the same level of overhead? How will you handle mergers and acquisitions with other companies this size and larger in your market space? You are starting to leave the micro business model and need have the ability to apply solid business practices to propel your company into the future. There is one thing that is certain, as you pass hurdles in the growth of your company there will always be competition.

N O T E S

N O T E S

2

DESIGN PHILOSOPHY

What's Inside

Your Mission Statement

Developing a Design Philosophy

Preparing Installation Kits

Golden Rules to Follow

Chapter Two

Introduction

Philosophy: unintelligible answers to insoluble problems.

– Henry Brooks Adams (1838–1918) US author, historian, son of Charles Francis Adams, grandson of John Quincy Adams

Running a residential integration business requires more than delivering and setting up home electronic systems. You must decide what equipment to select, know how it interacts with other equipment, how to install it, and anticipate how the customer will interact with it. Moreover for a successful business, you must determine who your customers are, what their core belief system is, and you must stick with your core values in making day–to–day decisions.

Whether you're focused on the latest technology while working on very few projects at a time, or aimed at providing easy–to–install products in tract homes, you must have a clear path delineating your direction. Your company's directors must develop a mission statement that provides the core values and direction of the company.

Design your organization to suit your specific type of business and customers. In other words embrace the concept that there is no one or correct way to grow your company. However, there are important steps that can not be overlooked. This book aims to teach those important steps.

Your chief engineer uses the mission statement to determine your company's design philosophy, which spells out how engineering in the company is to be handled. Lastly, your engineering staff creates installation standards for every product in the company.

We will take a look at a specific company, ABC inc., and how it arrives at what products and services to provide to its customers.

The Mission Statement

The mission statement is created by the company directors. It is used to measure day–to–day business decisions, and provides a clear view of what the company does for its customers. Without a mission statement the company's success is based on haphazard random luck. Although many theories exist regarding mission statements it is simply what you do for whom. **EVERYBODY** in the company should be able to quote it verbatim. Any additional concepts are included in bullet form beneath the statement as part of its core beliefs.

ABC inc.'s Mission Statement

ABC provides turnkey systems for entertainment, comfort, and convenience in the modern digital home.

Core Beliefs

ABC provides standardized, cost–effective, and high–performance systems to exceed our customer's expectations.

We agree to requirements and deliverables before work has begun, establish milestones and monitor progress throughout the project.

We strive to minimize on–site installation time.

From its mission statement ABC inc. decides to work the middle market, with systems that require a level of expertise beyond the capabilities of most homeowners. The company will provide repeatable systems that can be serviced by anyone in the company with minimal documentation of the specific system. Customers will have a consistent and happy experience with the company. Problems will rarely arise, and will be quickly solved. It is also concluded that the company would refrain from large custom projects, because they would require custom solutions that the company is not geared to handle.

The Design Philosophy

The design philosophy relates directly to a company's mission statement. It spells out engineering standards within the company, and is used to measure day–to–day engineering decisions. OK, so you have decided on the direction of the company which incorporates the overall direction, now you must make a second statement and focus it directly toward how the company systems will be designed. This is called the Design Philosophy.

ABC inc. Design Philosophy

All ABC inc. products must go through a thorough engineering process to determine what will be needed in each case: the required labor; the parts to connect the product to the system; and parts required for system–level control.

Each product must have: a written installation standard; a form designed to gather customer preferences; and a written process to train the customer.

Each product should use known and current technology that has a proven track record for being reliable, available, and serviceable. Each product must contain a programmable interface that allows for control from a remote location. Each product must have a lifespan of five years. ABC inc. will maintain facilities for development, production and testing of all customer systems prior to delivery.

In accordance with the mission statement, it is clear that products go through a formal process before becoming part of the company's menu. The company must be careful in reviewing possible products to ensure long–term availability.

The engineering staff goes through the above process to determine what products ABC inc. will provide to its customers.

The DVD Player as an Installation Kit

Your product is not what is purchased from your vendor, but what is sold to your customer. In accordance with the design philosophy, you must look at time costs of the delivered product.

Establish an appropriate amount of time for the in–house technician to install the product into the equipment rack and test. Consider the time for the field technician to install the rack in the cabinetry in your customer's home. Account for project management time, customer training, programming the user interface, and time to service the unit during the warranty period.

Now look at what parts are required to connect the component to the system. Decide what cables are required for the piece. Evaluate the difference between interconnects, such as component video, s–video, and composite, as well as analog audio and digital audio, both optical and coaxial cables. To provide a consistent video path through all sources, the engineer selects component video and coaxial digital audio cable. The equipment rack shelf is included as well as the required miscellaneous parts, such as cable ties and rack screws.

	DVD Player – Progressive Scan	*$220.27*
3	Project Management, minutes	16.25
43	In–House Technician, minutes	53.75
23	Field Technician, minutes	28.75
1	Xantech – 283M – Blink–IR Mouse Emitter, each	14.00
1	Ultralink – MDC–2M – 2 Meter Digital Coax Interconnect, pair	35.01
1	Ultralink – CCV–2M – 2 Meter Component Video Interconnect, each	72.51

Figure 2.1
DVD Player
Kit

Finally, look at the required parts to control the DVD player, see figure 2.1. You determine that infrared control is appropriate for this piece of gear. This decision is based upon what is available in the consumer market. However, only gear that has a discrete on/off IR control can be allowed. This means that there exists a remote control code to turn the unit both on as well as off. The only part required for control is an infrared emitter. Any additional control parts are included in the control system product. In addition, define a standard method for affixing and determining placement of the emitter.

The finished product consists of many resources, both product and time (labor). More importantly you have established a standard for all DVD players. This standard is one that is written in a manner that allows sales, installation, and engineering to understand exactly what is to be sold, and how it is to be installed. This standard is for a generic DVD player, and lists several brands and models that are acceptable. Therefore, the standard allows sales to determine the model based upon price point, brand awareness, and customer needs, and still ensures the DVD player will integrate with the overall system.

Now develop your product installation kits. Generally a kit will include everything — parts and labor costs — that is needed to install the product in your customer's home. In the case of the DVD player, your kit would include the items listed in the chart below. The actual DVD player is not part of the kit. It is priced separately because of market demand.

Pricing becomes difficult in the integrated home because you cannot simply buy a DVD player from a vendor, open the box and plug it into your customer's television set. That means you cannot compete with the prices of DVD players offered at discount stores. Your DVD player must be integrated into your customer's total system. So in order to keep your pricing at a level that is more palatable to your customer, you will have to shift some of the cost associated with the DVD player to other associated costs for the total integration. For example, you can include all the rack parts and associated supplies as part of the equipment rack that holds a number of pieces of equipment besides the DVD player. Figure 2.1 shows a list of parts and services required to install a DVD player, and figure 2.2 shows the housing for the equipment.

Pulling It All Together

We apply this process to every product that is sold by our company. Look at the audio processor and decide to select only models with an RS–232 port to ensure reliability and predictability. Carry out this process on all equipment within the home integration system, and continually revisit each product in the home integration system to ensure that it meets your company design philosophy. In the end

	Equipment Housing – Dual SR–SR2 Rack	*$2908.00*
480	Installation, finish phase, minutes	480.00
480	Cabinetry Design, minutes	480.00
1	Panamax – Max 8 surge protector, each	49.00
2	Middle Atlantic — SRSR–2 rotating and sliding rack system, each	976.00
4	Middle Atlantic — LB–1R horizontal lacing bar, each	28.00
4	Middle Atlantic — RSH–4S custom racking shelf, each	498.00
6	Middle Atlantic — EVT–1 one-space vent panel , each	59.00
1	Elan — ZFANR rack mount fan, each	249.00
63	Miscellaneous project supplies, dollars	64.00
180	Project Management, minutes	225.00

Figure 2.2 Equipment Rack Kit

a standard evolves that can be used by all departments in our company to formulate day–to–day decisions, such as how to bid, design, install, and service each project.

Golden Rules

I Pray Heaven to bestow the best of blessing on THIS HOUSE, and on All that shall hereafter Inhabit it. May none but honest and wise men ever rule under this roof!

– John Adams (1735–1826) 2nd US president 1797–1801, 1st vice president 1789–97, strong revolutionary leader

Over the years we have formulated some golden rules of business. These are included below. There are many more, however, these represent a few of the more important ones.

The "Largest Customer" Rule

Don't accept any project that you can't afford to lose mid project. If your largest customer got angry and cancelled the project, would your company be able to withstand the problems it would create?

Many years ago our company was at $300,000 in annual revenue. We sold a project that was $300,000 in revenue. This was going to be great! It represented a whole year's revenue. Just imagine our excitement over one single project that was going to double our annual sales.

We geared up. We hired a couple of people, and developed a rather large design document for our wonderful $300,000 project, and gave it to our customer. We practically reinvented our company — all to meet the needs of our wonderful $300,000 project. A few days before we were scheduled to start cabling for our $300,000 project, the customer terminated us. Yes, terminated us. Apparently the customer had taken our design document, put it out to bid, and found someone else to do it for less money. We were in a tail–spin. We went from the exhilaration of doubling our sales to almost going out of business. It took us more than a year to recuperate from the loss of our "wonderful $300,000 project."

Stick to this rule, and if the job gets canceled or delayed, it won't have a serious impact on your company's income.

Another way to look at it is to limit your electronics time. How do you determine your electronics time? The electronics time is half the termination time, and the termination time is half the cabling time. We explain in more detail in the structured wiring chapter of this book. No customer is going to want you in their home after they start living there for more than a week. It may be possible that they might tolerate you being there for two weeks. You have to ask yourself, can our company complete the electronics time in less than two weeks. If the project that represents six to seven months of your income, it is very doubtful. Basically, you really can't. And as you hang out on the job longer and longer, your customer is likely to lose respect for your work simply because it's taking so long. So remember a very important rule is the "Largest Customer" rule.

The "Outsource It" Rule

Don't accept more work than you can handle internally, and outsource whatever makes sense. This does not mean turning away work, but instead you should plan. Work your business window farther out, and PLAN your capacity accordingly.

An example of outsourcing is calibration of video projectors. Let's say you're selling one video projector a month. How could you possibly be great at calibrating that projector? You're probably just OK, if you only do it once a month. Also consider this. Does it make sense to buy $5,000 worth of test tools, to calibrate one projector a month? The return on investment is insignificant, if there is any return at all. What is much better to do is to find an expert, who calibrates projectors full time. Then you contract with that person, now your subcontractor.

You'll need to write a set of guidelines so that there's a clear delineation of the subcontractor's responsibility and your responsibility. In this book's download, we've included a host of subcontractor agreements that you can use.

Consider hiring the following types of subcontractors::

Calibration Expert — to calibrate video and audio consumer electronics

Satellite Installer — to install the dish and cables to the attic

IT (Information Technology) Expert — to configure your customer's computers

Electrician — to provide a host of electrical services outside the limits of your company

Drapery Installer — to install the motorized drapes

HVAC Installer — to deal with the complex HVAC issues when they come up

Cabinetmakers — to design and build cabinetry

You can use subcontractors until your company has grown to the point that you can create a full-time position to perform that role.

Temporary partnerships are another avenue you can take in meeting your customer's needs. You might be able to find someone who is an excellent lighting control designer and programmer. You can establish an informal partnership with that person. In the partnership, you sell and install the lighting control system, and they provide the documentation and programming. And they work with the on-site electrician to make sure everything is installed properly. That's how you create a partnership. When your company grows large enough to need a full-time lighting control employee, then you can end that partnership, and hire someone internally. Taking this kind of approach will help you to build a larger and stable company.

Look for subcontractors to run your cables. Consider creating a relationship with a local electrician or security dealer, who can cable your customers' homes, and know your specifications. Perhaps they could even supply the cabling. Keep in mind that cabling is a critical part of your offerings and you should only outsource for as long as necessary to grow your company.

Start to look at subcontractors meshed with your company employees to give your customers all the services they need and want. Combining the practice of hiring subcontractors and full–time employees will allow your internal workforce to grow naturally and not before your company is ready.

The "What NOT to Automate" Rule

Customers will ask you automate a host of things. If you listen to them, and automate those things, you could create potential legal issues you might have to deal with in the future. Here's an example. One dealer agreed to control a gas fireplace from a touchscreen. Those controls were made available throughout the home. This story is from a friend, who was running tech support for the manufacturer involved. The manufacturer wound up being sued because of the automated gas fireplace. The customer's children were playing in the fireplace in the living room. Not where you would expect children to play, but they were. Someone in another part of the home accidentally activated the fireplace through the touchscreen. The child was burned. It wasn't serious, but he was burned slightly on his legs and arms. He recovered, thankfully with no scaring but he did receive a hefty scare and had to be taken to the hospital.

The result: the dealer was sued, and the manufacturer was sued. And nobody was happy. When you're automating, you need to think about safety.

Some items not to automate:

- Motorized chandeliers, garage doors
- Fireplaces, swimming pools
- Spas or other heated water devices
- Anything else that is motorized

Be very careful how you automate. Only provide a control for a motorized device that you can see from the location of the touchscreen. Garage doors open and close only when you physically point the remote at the garage door. You can't do it from a distance. And the buttons are inside the garage door, not in the family room where the person closing the door wouldn't be able to see the door.

It might sound cool to be able to close a garage door from the bedroom at the end of the day, but garage doors are mechanical. You'd run the risk of damage to property and people — even though the door is supposed to stop if it hits something half way down. As a result you could put yourself out of business trying to avoid a court settlement.

There are many other things that you should question how advisable it would be to automate. In making your decision, ask yourself the following:

- Is this something that should be automated?
- What is the purpose of the automation?
- Is this being done for a cool factor? ("It would be really cool to automate ...")

You have a greater responsibility to your employees, their families, your vendors and your customers as a whole, than a single customer.

The "Design with Backups" Rule

Everything that you design for your customer should have some sort of manual override or backup system. Let's look at some examples.

If you're going to install automated thermostats, the appropriate way is to first select a thermostat. We recommend a good model, and provide installation information in the chapter, "HVAC Integration". Basically, you select a model of a thermostat that works and acts very similar to every other thermostat that your customer might purchase for their home.

During the installation, let's say you put the thermostats in the basement and run a temperature sensor into each room in the house. You have taken the thermostat out of the room, and changed the way the room was originally designed. It also removes any possibility of a manual backup. If the integrated system goes down, your customer will have no way to operate the thermostats.

A better way is to leave the thermostat installed in the room. Now the customer can use the thermostat the way he/she normally would, and integration will add enhanced, layered capability. If the customer does not want the thermostat on a wall in the room because of the decor, you can install it in a nearby closet, and run a temperature sensor to the room itself.

Say you're in the master suite; we suggest you put the thermostat right inside the entrance of the master walk-in closet. That way the walls in the master suite are left uncluttered. And you can install a temperature sensor in the master suite and connect it to the thermostat in the master closet. For the convenience of your customer, remember to label the thermostat, with the name of the room that it controls, i.e. master bedroom thermostat.

Motorized shades and drapes also should be designed with a manual switch when planning your integrated system. We recommend that you first install 110-volt switches to operate individual shades and drapes. When your customer turns on the power, the drapes open, or the shades go up; and when your customer turns off the power, the drapes close, or the shades go down. This allows the homeowner to walk over to a switch to operate the shades and drapes without the integration system.

Now adding the drapes and shades to the integrated system extends and enhances the capability of the motorized system. By connecting the shades and drapes to a "Smart Switch", the homeowner can touch a button on a keypad or a touchscreen, and the drapes and shades will respond to a pre-determined lighting scene. For example, a homeowner could press "Home", and the drapes or shades would open in response to the request. If the integration system is unable to transmit instructions for any reason, your customer still could operate the drapes and shades from the 110–volt switches.

The lighting control system is another system that should have a manual backup capability. Everyone knows what an electrical light switch is, and most people know what a dimmer switch is. They've been around since electrical switches were first designed. Suppose you take all of those light switches that would normally be installed in each room of your customer's home, and install them on a panel in the basement. Then you connect them to a computer in the basement to control them. And connect the computer to keypads in each room for the customer to use. What would happen in an emergency? You're right. The entire system would go down. You would have taken away your customer's ability go to each room and turn on and off the lights. And, in addition, the homeowner's guests may have trouble trying to figure out how to turn on or off the light.

Now suppose you're in a room where décor again is important, and there is a room that needs a lot of light switches for various reasons. The dilemma is solved by installing the two main dimmers, i.e. the dimmers for recessed ceiling lights and the chandelier, at the entrance to the room. The dimmers for supplementary lights can be installed in a closet. Supplementary lighting could include lighting to highlight artwork, cove lighting at windows, bookshelf lighting, or other specialty lighting. Remember to label each dimmer located in a closet with its function, i.e. artwork lighting, master bedroom.

If the integration system goes down, your customer still can enter a room, and hit the light dimmer at the entrance to turn on the lights. Or walk to a closet and turn on a dimmer.

What if we take a different approach? Suppose it's Christmas Eve, and there's a failure in the lighting control system. And you've designed a centralized system. In other words, the cables for all your dimmers go down to the basement and connect to a panel that is controlled by a computer. That single failure somewhere in the system will take down all the lighting throughout the home — just like old–fashioned Christmas tree lights. When one went out, they all went out. And you had to check them all to find out which was the faulty light.

In our example, your customer is left sitting in the dark— in a multi-million home. And that customer cannot use the home until you service that system. So your customer and family head for the Four Seasons, at your expense. Now you're servicing a customer on Christmas Eve, trying to resolve a major problem. You're not at home enjoying the holiday with your family, so your family is not happy; your customer's not happy; and you're not happy. It's a lose-lose situation.

In an integration system design, it is better to include in-line dimmers (dimmers that connect directly from the wall switch to the light), and also connect to the integrated system. If a lighting system designed this way goes down, your customer still could go to those dimmers and turn on and off the lights manually. All they would lose is the capability to select house-wide lighting scenes. Granted it's not perfect, but it will save you from that last-minute service call, and allow the customer to use their home during the time you're serving the system.

Many years later, your customer still will own his/her lighting control system. And if you get into a situation where a single dimmer fails, you will be able to replace it with a single dimmer switch, or pay an electrical contractor a few dollars to fix it. That's a far easier scenario, than replacing the entire lighting system. Think about these kinds of issues when you design every system in the home.

Consider:

- Does it have a manual override?
- Does it have a backup system?
- Is it designed for future repairs?

It is also important to remember that 10 years down the road, parts may no longer be available for the system you installed. In that case, installing dimmers separately in each room will make it easier for you to replace broken dimmers. If a specific dimmer is no longer made, you can move a dimmer from a little–used room to one that has heavier traffic. Ordinary dimmers that are not connected to the integrated systems can be installed in the little–used room. Then at some point, your customer may want to begin replacing his/her lighting control system with a newer model. But he/she temporarily could use the original integrated lighting system for the rooms with the appropriate "Smart Switches".

The "Partner with Your Vendor" Rule

As a small businessman, it's important for you to develop strong partnerships with your vendors. By stacking up your purchases with fewer vendors, you gain more power and flexibility with the vendors and your customers. There always will be times when products fail, and you will need to call upon your vendors for their help. If you deal with large vendors for which you are an insignificant customer, it is unlikely that you will get the help you need.

Look to your vendors for support such as marketing, training cooperative advertising, and other support programs; however it is equally important to understand you must do your part. Help them succeed by not creating undo burdens financially or otherwise. You work with them and they will work with you.

To develop a good relationship with a vendor, sell the same products to all your customers. For example, sell the same brand DVD player every time. Pick a brand that has a good reputation for long life, and can meet your customers' needs. Your repeat business can help you form a strong partnership with that DVD vendor.

Don't fall into the trap of buying the "latest and greatest", and bouncing from vendor to vendor. And don't let your customer dictate to you which products to supply. You'll wind up buying from far too many vendors, and never manage the integration process to your benefit. The bottom line for your business is not whose DVD player you provide, but is the DVD player reliable, can it be serviced and can it be installed smoothly.

If the DVD player can do all that, then you've found a vendor with whom it's worth developing a good relationship and partnership.

NOTES

NOTES

N O T E S

3

BEFORE THE PROJECT STARTS

What's Inside

Creating Computer Files

Using an Intranet

Creating Manual Files

Chapter Three

Introduction

Unless you're willing to have a go, fail miserably, and have another go, success won't happen.

– Phillip Adams Australian author, broadcaster, film–maker, newspaper columnist, writer, producer, editor, critic

In this chapter we will discuss what has to happen within your company before formally opening a home integration project.

Much of the administrative procedures will depend upon the size of your company. Larger companies will require more structure, while smaller companies can tolerate less.

Your company's sales people, of course, provide the initial contract with a potential customer. The sales person listens to the customer to gather information about what that customer is looking for in an integrated system. That information becomes the blueprint for the first version of your proposal.

You present that version to your customer, and invariably, he/she will want some changes. Incorporating the changes into the first proposal becomes the second version. This can go on for several meetings until the customer is satisfied with the proposal and agrees to sign a contract.

It is very important that you keep a copy of every version of your proposal to your customer for two reasons. The first reason is you need to use the most current proposal in talking with your customer. The second reason is so you can access an earlier version, if your customer decides he/she likes something in that earlier version.

A simple way to ensure proper version control is create a PDF (portable document format) file with a name, a proposal number, a version number and the date – every time you release another version of a proposal to your customer.

Setting up the File Server

In order to track proposals, open projects, closed project, and all of the leads use the file structure shown in figure 3.1. The following assumes your server is named "Server"

```
\\Server
        \In Service Customers          (customers in service period)
                \Adams, Ansel          (current project files)
                        \OLD           (All previous versions)
                \Adams, Scott

                ...

                \Yang, Ying
        \Leads                         (customer leads)
                \Adams, Barney         (current project files)
                        \OLD           (All previous versions)
                \Adams, Fred

                ...

                \Zoolander, Timmi
        \Project Templates             (proposals, memos, etc.)
                \OLD                   (All previous versions)
        \Open Customers                (customers with an open
                                        project)
                \Adams, John           (current project files)
                        \OLD           (All previous versions)
                \Adams, Samuel

                ...

                \Zabrinsky, Fred
        \Out Of Service Customers      (customers out of service
                                        period)
                \Adams, Douglas        (current project files)
                        \OLD           (All previous versions)
                \Adams, Franklin

                ...

                \Yang, Ying
```

Figure 3.1
File
Structure

On your computer network at your business, you can create a folder on your main hard disc, and call it "Open projects". Inside the "Open projects" folder you have sub-folders, each with a customer name. Inside the customer sub-folders you would have all of the key documents and information required for that project. Everyone on each team can work on their own computer and access the folders, subfolders, and files for your customers. When someone releases a new version of a document, it can be stored on the main hard disc. In this way the files can be shared among all the team members. Also remember to add a document number, version number, customer name, and date to each new release of any document.

The files in the subfolders could be cabinet drawings, proposal versions, building materials, change orders, or a variety of other pertinent documents.

Your most current files should be the ones easiest to access. To keep your main folder uncluttered, you can create a subfolder named "old". You can move any of the older versions of information to the "old" subfolder. Do not delete them. If you have a new version of a cabinet drawing, take the previous version and move it to "old". This system allows you to go back into "old" and check pervious versions as necessary, and keeps the current files in the main folder.

Also keep each file in a PDF format. Suppose you're doing your cabinet drawing, you would have a 2D–CAD document and, in addition, you would have a PDF copy of all files for easy retrieval. Not everyone is going to have your 2D–CAD software installed on their computer at work, but most have a PDF reader installed.

Naming the Proposal Files

There are four documents for each proposal: a WORD document, an EXCEL document, and a PDF version of each. The word document contains the proposal text and the EXCEL document contains the pricing information. In addition there should be a PDF version of each file that has been released to the customer. Go to the appropriate proposal directory and get the next number in sequence and label the files as such;

The proposal number is 101, the customer name is Adams, Douglas (abbreviated ADAMD from the first four letters of the last name and the first letter of the first) and the template is the Digital Home. This is the first revision of the proposal.

0101ADAMDV01 Digital Home Proposal.doc

0101ADAMDV01 Digital Home Pricing.xls

0101ADAMDV01 Digital Home Proposal.pdf

0101ADAMDV01 Digital Home Pricing.pdf

If the customer requests changes to the proposal then the version number becomes 02, 03, and so on. Once the proposal is accepted and there are change orders, the first digit is incremental and the second becomes 1. So the first revision of the first change order reads 11, then it is incremented as 12, 13, until accepted.

Finally, your customer agrees to the final proposal. You are almost ready to formally open your project.

But before you open any project, you need two more items. You still need to receive a check from your customer and you need a signed contract that incorporates your final proposal. Do not open any project without those two critical items: a signed contract from the customer and a check for the initial payment.

Creating Project Folders

At this point, you are ready to formally open the project. Meet with your team, and have your company office administrator open the project. That person will prepare multiple folders in various colors for your various installation teams. He/she prepares a folder for engineering, one for installation, one for project management, one for sales, and one for administration. This will depend on the organization and size of your company, as outlined in the introduction chapter of this book. A copy of the final proposal and other appropriate information goes inside each one of these folders. Figure 3.2 Contains list of files that go in each folder. Depending on the size of your company you might have one file marked engineering & installation. But as your company grows, you'll probably want to create separate files for both functions.

Color and Purpose	A	B	C	D	E	F	G
Blue – Admin	X	X			X		
Red – Sales	X		X		X		
Green – PM	X		X	X		X	X
Yellow – Install	X			X		X	
Brown – Eng.	X		X	X		X	X

A – Proposal and all accepted revisions

B – Copy of signed contract and copies of checks

C – Project memos

D – Bill of materials (BOM), by phase with quantities

E – BOM with pricing

F – Cabintery, theater, and other drawings

G – Lighting control documents

Figure 3.2
File
Folders

Building an Intranet

As your company grows, you may want to take organizing your folders on computer to the next level. A good way to do it is through a company called **www.intranets.com**. Signing up for this service allows you to have an on–the–web intranet site to share information.

You can assign everyone in your company, as well as your customers and other contractors (the architect, the builder, and others) to the intranet site. Once they have an account, you can give them permission to access the folders on the intranet. They can go in and view the documents that pertain to them, and those documents can exist there during that project. And of course, these permissions can be given as read only to ensure the original data is not changed.

It's a good way to manage all of your information. And your main role as integrators is management. You're not physically doing a lot of the work, you hire installers for that. But what you're going to be doing is managing and organizing the work, and making sure everyone is informed. Having an intranet will be invaluable in organizing the work, however it is best to have a full–time office manager who can do the uploads and do the maintenance of intranet. Actually in our opinion, it's less work than managing the folders, and the information is retrievable from a laptop anywhere in the world. And keeps it secured. But it requires a level of discipline that is hard to come by in smaller companies.

The "General Contractor" Letter

Dear Sirs;

(Company Name) values the relationship between the Homeowner, General Contractor and Subcontractors. In order to exceed our customers' expectations work is sometimes required of others to complete our product. We have advised our customer that there are extra services needed, as outlined below, that are not included in our pricing. These services should be billed directly to the homeowner.

Although we have outlined many of the items that are not included in our contract, there may be other items that arise during the construction process. We would recommend each of these issues be discussed with the customer and all involved to create the right action plan.

(Company Name) responsibilities

We will cable, install, terminate, and finish all Telephone, TV, Satellite, Phone System, Computer, Music System, and Theater items as contracted.

We will maintain workman's compensation through out the complete project.

We will acquire all necessary permits and observe all national and local building codes.

We will provide specification of all contracted equipment installed with built–in cabinetry.

NOTES

By sending this letter to the general contractor, and a copy to the customer you are letting everyone know what you will and won't do.

It is important to not ony send the letter but discuss these items with the contractor. Your tone should always be helpful and pleasent. And just as important be careful on what you agree to take on. If the builder can't or won't work with you on these items, talk with your customer and ask for help.

We will install all finished equipment after the customer has taken possession of the home. This may take up to 60 days depending on the complexity of the system.

What We Need You To Do

- Provide various electrical outlets where needed for auxiliary devices throughout the home. These locations are often needed for Televisions, Computer peripherals, Telephone chargers etc... These locations will be laid out during the rough electrical walk thru or as specified on the plans.

- Provide two dedicated 20 Amp services in the basement located at main panel for telephone, television, music, and networking.

- Provide conduit to the street for Telephone and CATV services.

- Provide conduit for use for exterior speakers or connections to exterior buildings.

- Provide a wood panel to accommodate the equipment in the basement and needed floor area for the equipment.

- Cut–in all of our devices that will be installed in custom cabinetry, baseboard molding, and other finished woodwork.

We need to be involved with the cabinet designs that will house our equipment. We will need wiring access, ventilation, and power for the installed equipment. We are therefore requesting to be copied on all cabinetry design; in addition we request final approval before any of this cabinet is built.

We request that you schedule and communicate with us throughout the construction process of the home. We would also request a fair and reasonable time to complete all the steps in our process.

Thank You,

(PM Name)

(Title and Contact Information)

NOTES

NOTES

4

STRUCTURED WIRING

What's Inside

Chapter Four

What is Structured Wiring

We cannot advance without new experiments in living, but no wise man tries every day what he has proved wrong the day before.

– James Truslow Adams (1878–1949) American essayist & historian

Although the industry uses the term structured wiring, it is in fact all cable. In this book we will refer to wire as cable when the word stands alone

The structured wiring system is the most important system in the integrated home, and it also is the largest chapter in our book. It lays the foundation for every other system that we will be discussing.

Much of your attention should be put toward the organization of the structured wiring system. The more organized and well thought out this system is, the easier the other systems will be to install and service at a later date.

An example of this is your telephone system. If you install your phone system with disorganized cabling and panels, when you attempt to repair a problem in the phone system, you could spend days and days trying to resolve it. If you design your structured wiring system properly, your panels are labeled properly, and your cables are color coded, then when it comes time to service the telephone system, you'll resolve the issue in short order. This will go a long way in building customer confidence.

In properly planning the structured wiring system, it is essential to build a distribution panel in every project. For every type of wallplate that you install, you need a distribution panel. The distribution panel can be configured in various sizes depending on the number of wallplates in the home. The distribution panels discussed in this book are designed for homes of 5,000 square feet or larger; designed for maximum serviceability; and designed for the type of features that high–end homes demand. If you are working in smaller homes, you might want to scale down your panels.

As you cable the home, you will find every cable has a different color code. It is extremely important to keep them well organized. The different color cables allow you to cable the home quickly, and very easily terminate and test them with little discussion between sales and installation.

Suppose you are using all grey cat5e cables for all electronic functions throughout the home. After cabling the home what you wind up with is a pile of grey cat5e cables. You won't know how to terminate each one of those cables. You will need to tone and label them in order to be able to terminate them. If you have different color cables – white for telephone, blue for networking – you can literally terminate the cables based on the color of the cable. That means you won't need to put labels on the cables to identify them. Labels can tear or come off before you've had a chance to complete the termination phase.

We recommend that you use white cat5e cables for telephones, and terminate them in the basement with a white RJ45, terminated to the T568B standard. Then snap them into the telephone distribtuion panel. Do the same thing with the networking cables, execpt use blue cables and blue RJ45 connectors. Continue using different color cables for all the different functions of the systems.

Test each cable run and when it passes, label it. In this way the label signifies that the cable has passed test as well as identifying the function. It's a great feeling to walk into a job and see a cable that is labeled and know it's passed test. If you see cables that are terminated and not labeled, they have failed test or crew hasn't tested yet. That means you can call back the termination crew to finish their work. Color coding helps to minimize the need for communication between teams and allows everyone to focus on the big picture of meeting the customer's needs.

Color coding is critical in terms of working with multiple crews.

If you have the same crew working from cabling to trim out, that's good. They will understand the job. But as your company grows, you might not always get the same crew. So by defining the specific standards on how the cables are going to be terminated and how they are going to be labeled, you will make it very simple for multiple crews to go into the job, very quickly understand what needs to be done, and come up to speed.

We will discuss how to run the cables, how to terminate the cables, how to test the cables, how to label the cables, and how to color code the cables. Finally, we will discuss how to get the home ready for the move-in day.

What it does not include are the actual electronic devices, such as the television, telephone, or computer. When we pop in the phone system, it will literally just plug into the distribution panel in the basement and the wallplates upstairs. You can put in a phone system in a couple of hours, based on the heavy work you did in the structured wiring installation.

The other remaining item to be installed after the customer moves in is the music system. All you'll need to install are the keypads and speakers. This goes very smoothly as all of the connections and cables have been terminated, tested, and labeled. Simply deliver the pre-built equipment rack, plug it into a pre-set bundle of cables, and your done!

Your electronics crew does not need to know anything about the home or how the cables are run. All the crew needs to do is show up with the equipment rack. And know the color coding scheme for the cables, and trust that if a cable is labeled it has passed test. All that is left is to literally plug in the rack and plug in the speakers. You can install a $40,000 music system in a single day. Very profitable, and it all goes back to a highly defined, well organized structured wiring system.

Figure 3.1 show the typical wiring for a kitchen. The Multimedia wallplate is located at the kitchen desk, while the "Telephone &

Networking" wallplate is at outlet hieght next to the kitchen table for a quick plug–in for homework. The Touchscreen provides control of the lighting, HVAC, and music in the room, as well the entire home.

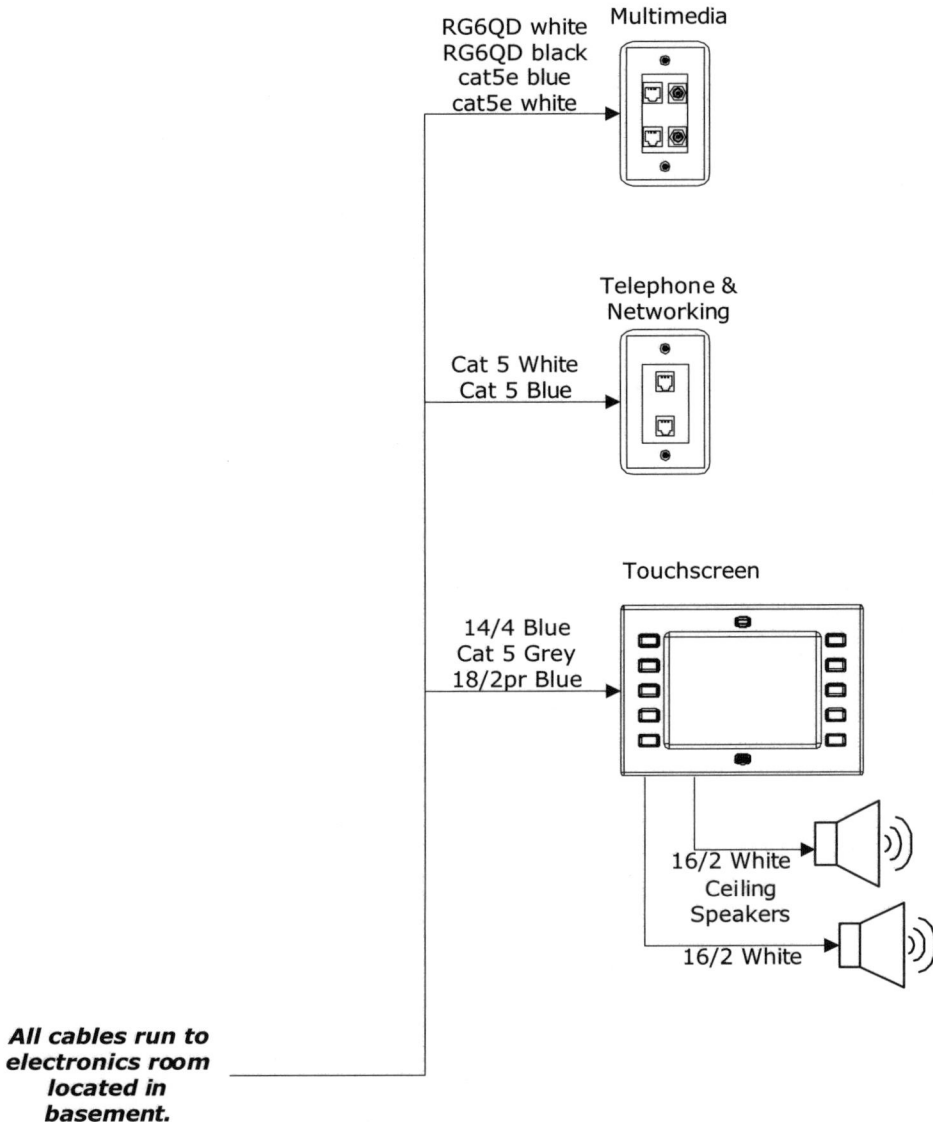

RG6QD white
RG6QD black
cat5e blue
cat5e white

Multimedia

Telephone &
Networking

Cat 5 White
Cat 5 Blue

Touchscreen

14/4 Blue
Cat 5 Grey
18/2pr Blue

16/2 White
Ceiling
Speakers
16/2 White

All cables run to electronics room located in basement.

Figure 4.1
Wiring diagram for
typical kitchen

Customer Proposal

NOTES

The cusomter proposal text lays out what specifically your company will provide the customer.

It explains the details in easy-to-understand terms and leaves out the technology jargon.

Don't attempt to impress your customers with your technical exptertise, instead be clear and consise.

Present the proposal and all revsions in person and explain each system as you present.

To meet our ever–increasing demands for technology at home, a broad range of communication and multimedia services must be available throughout our homes. Telephone, home networks, Internet, cable television, satellite, and high definition television – all these elements of consumer electronics have special cabling requirements we call structured wiring. Structured wiring lays the foundation that allows your technology devices to work together to make your daily life convenient and more pleasurable.

As part of a structured wiring plan for your home, we have designed wallplates and panels that allow us to connect the necessary cables in your home to the integration system. At the wallplates and panels, which are installed in key locations that you help select in your home, you receive immediate access to:

Broadband Internet.

Shared files, printers, and other online resources on all your computers.

Multiple telephone lines.

High–definition signals for Off–Air (traditional TV), Satellite and Cable.

Home–wide music system.

Our Certified Installers will meet every requirement of the EIA/TIA 570A Residential Wiring Specifications.

Wallplates

NOTES

The telephone only wallplate is very seldom used. The wallplate used in most locations is the telephone & networking wallplate.

The Multimedia wallplate is great for bedrooms, the study, and anywhere the customer may want to put a television.

Use the Surround Sound wallplate in the family room, or anyplace that may receive a surround system in the future.

By placing the music wallplates in the structured wiring section you lay the foundation for a music system; and you also keep pricing at a minimum for that section.

It is always a good idea to spread out pricing to avoid to sticker shock to your customer.

You can choose wallplates with our standard colors of white, ivory, almond, and black, or you can select wallplates with one of the special finishes that are available. Our wallplates fit the décor of any home. You can select any number or combinations of the wallplates listed below.

Hanging Telephone Wallplate – The hanging telephone wallplate allows connections for two (2) telephone lines.

Telephone & Networking Wallplate – The telephone & networking wallplate allows connections to four (4) telephone lines and a home network.

Multimedia Wallplate – The multimedia wallplate allows connection to cable television, satellite, four (4) telephone lines, and a home network.

Surround Sound Wallplate – The surround sound wallplate allows for two (2) connections to cable television, two (2) connections to satellite, connections to four (4) telephone lines, your home network, your home–wide stereo, your home–wide integration system, and also cabling for surround sound speakers.

Music & Video Output Wallplate – The music & video output wallplate sends a music and video signal from the main entertainment center to the location of the wallplate.

Music & Video Input Wallplate – The music & video input wallplate sends a music and video signal from the wallplate location to the main

73

entertainment center.

Speaker Cabling – Speaker cables that are included are enough to cable one pair of architectural speakers.

Speaker Wallplate – The speaker wallplate includes cabling for one pair of speakers and a wallplate suitable for connecting bookshelf speakers.

Distribution Panels

You can select a variety of distribution panels from those listed below. Media panels are generally located in an electronics closet in the basement.

System Telephone & Home Networking Media Panel – Designed to connect the telephone system, home networking switches, and routers to the wallplates. This panel is clearly labeled for easy customer changes.

Cable Television Panel – Designed to bring a sharp, clear picture to every television in your home, using a radio frequency (RF) amplifier. In addition, by using integrated infrared technology, it allows you to control your DVD player, satellite receiver, digital cable box, or any other audio/video device and all your televisions. Just point and click your handheld remote control at the compact infrared (IR) box on any of your televisions. The IR box sends a signal to a central location (often in your basement) and it instantly obeys your command. The IR technology also allows you to share a satellite signal or one cable box among several televisions, and allows you to

NOTES

If you provide any of the wallplates from the previous section you must provide the appropriate distribution panel.

The Cable Television panel designed here is based around Channel Plus technology, but can easily be reworded to accommodate your current line of RF amplifiers.

Keeping the HD satellite panel, dish and cables part of this section allows you to market price the receivers, while retaining margins.

You should include the Off–Air panel on every job that requires FM reception. Keep in mind it sends the signal through the HD satellite panel.

keep unsightly cable boxes in your basement and not on top of each television.

High Definition Digital Satellite Panel – Includes a 21-inch satellite dish and a multiswitch that takes the high definition satellite signal and distributes it equally to televisions throughout your home.

Off-Air High Definition Television (HDTV) and FM Reception Panel – Includes an unseen digital antenna for off-air HDTV and FM reception. Reception is dependent on the location of your home and actual channels will vary.

Customer Information

The table below shows each wallplate in your home. We will field locate each wallplate in the rooms shown below with a "cabling" sticker. This will give you an opportunity to approve all locations before the home is cabled.

NOTES

The table to the right represents a sample customer worksheet. By having these tables at the back of each written proposal section you can quickly tailor the system to your customer's needs without reinventing the wheel within your proposal system.

The numbers indicate where and how many wallplates the customer wants installed throughout his/her home.

The template on the download contains columns for music wallplates and speaker cabling.

Location	Telephone & Networking	Television	Multimedia	Surround Sound
Kitchen	1		1	
Breakfast Rm				
Study	1		1	
Living Rm	1			
Dining Rm				
Family Rm	2			1
Deck				
Garage	1			
Master Bdrm	2		1	
Master Bath	1			
Bedroom 2			1	
Bedroom 3			1	
Bedroom 4			1	
Theater Rm	1			1
Game Rm	1		1	
Totals	11	1	8	2

Figure 4.1
Wallplate
Locations

Distribution Panel	Capacity
Telephone & Networking	24
Television	15
High Definition Satellite	16
Off Air HDTV & FM Reception	16

Figure 4.2
Media Panel
Capacities

Cabling Best Practices

The following list of Best Practices is recommended reading before the start of each new project. Gradually, you will remember most of them, and it will only be necessary to briefly review the list. It is always advisable to read the list regularly. Following these tips will save you time and money by "doing it right" the first time.

- Separate cables from power wiring (do not run side by side). See table below for minimum distance between telecommunications cable and all power sources to prevent interference (see figure 3.3).

Power source	Minimum separation
Bare power or light	Five (5) feet
Electrical supply cables not over 300V	Two (2) inches
Any transmission cables in conduit, or in armored or non–metallic sheath cable/power ground cables	Two (2) inches
Radio and/ or TV antenna lead and ground cables without grounded shield	Four (4) inches
Signal or control cables not over 300V	Two (2) inches
Community television systems coaxial cables with grounded shield	Two (2) inches
Telephone cables	Two (2) inches
Neon Signs and associated cabling from transformer	Six (6) inches
Fluorescent lighting cables	Five (5) inches
Lighting rods and cables	Six (6) feet

Figure 4.3
Cable
Seperations

- Avoid splicing cables on cable runs. If you make a mistake, pull a new cable.

- Limit "pulling tension" on 4–pair cables to no more than 25 pounds. Follow manufacturer's directions for pulling larger capacity cables.

- Avoid sharp bends in cable.

- Avoid nicking the protective sheath covering the cables.

- Use plastic, non–metallic staples to support cable.

• Leave cable loose inside the staples. Driving staples in tightly will crimp and damage the cable, impairing its capability of carrying voice/data. The cable may pass when it is tested with a cable–mapping device, but when a keypad or other device is attached to the cable; it will fail the same test.

• Maintain polarity (i.e. carefully match cable colors) of the Tip (+) and Ring (–) pairs from the demarcation point to the outlets. Polarity reversal causes problems with some telephones and most data devices.

• When a conduit is installed, always leave a pull cord to make it easier to run new cable.

• Avoid at all times running power cables and telecommunication cables in the same conduit. The only lines that may share conduit with telecommunications are low–voltage monitor and control lines.

• Try to avoid running cables under carpet because the cables can be more easily damaged especially in a private residence. When the only option available is to install the cable under carpet, follow the manufacturer's directions carefully.

• Allow only a single transition from one type of cabling to another for one room, a standard practice.

• Always avoid installing under carpet runs in damp areas.

• Please note that under carpet power cables are prohibited in residential installations.

• Try to run cables in inner walls to avoid conflict with firebreaks and insulation. It is also a lot easier to replace or add cables (if necessary) in inner walls. When you absolutely cannot avoid installing cables in external wall, follow the same method used in the installation of electrical cable.

• Allow adequate distance between signal cabling and power cabling when the cables are run parallel. When the distance is insufficient, cross the cables at 90° angles, and never allow signal cables to share bore holes with power cables.

• Keep cable away from sources of heat, such as hot water pipes, heater ducts and glass walls subject to direct sunlight.

• Avoid running cables outside a building, especially in new construction – it is unattractive and poses safety issues. Local wiring codes may, however, allow outside cables for additions to the original construction.

• Leave eighteen (18) inches of spare cable at outlets and connection points to allow for possible new connections and changes.

• Leave thirty–six (36) inches of spare cable at distribution panels.

• Use nail plates when drilling within one (1) inch of the face of any stud.

Tools & Supplies

Installation of telecommunication cables and equipment uses that are used for general electrical installations. Listed below are some of the frequently–used tools and supplies. However, you may need to expand the list. We are making recommendations of specific brands and models that we know will work well. Use your own judgment in seeking equivalent tools and supplies, as many do exist.

Cabling Tools

Dewalt makes several 18V cordless kits that are excellent for the cabling phase. You will need the following items as part of the kit you choose.

- 1/2" hammer drill driver (They make a 24V version that is excellent, but currently it is not part of a kit. You may want to consider buying it as a second drill.)
- Circular saw, which allows you to cut strapping, 2x4s, and ply-wood.
- Reciprocating saw to get into places the circular saw does not allow.
- Flexible floodlight, which will be invaluable.
- Extra batteries.

When you have assembled your kit, take a small piece of plywood and on it mount two battery rechargers and a power strip. Then wrap an extension cord around the plywood. This setup will allow you to continually recharge your tools when they are not in use. Avoid leaving uncharged batteries in your truck or van, and never leave them in cold temperatures. Nothing is more frustrating than arriving at the job on time, and then needing to wait to charge your tools.

You will need fiberglass step ladders of several sizes. We recommend four–foot, six–foot, eight–foot, and twelve–foot ladders. We recommend using a ladder that is rated for at least 300 lbs. Green

Bull Ladders, **www.greenbullladders.com**, makes many excellent models from which to choose.

Small Tools

You will also need various hand tools, such as a linesman pliers, hammer, razor blade, various screwdrivers, Allen–head driver, and similar tools. You can find these items as well as an appropriate tool box at Home Depot. **www.homedepot.com** We recommend using the gift cards from Home Depot in $50 amounts for small tools. Simply give each employee a gift card each year to maintain the required small tools, and don't expect these small tools to be returned upon an employee's exit from the company. For large value tools; print your company name and number on each tool and count them at the quarterly inventory.

Supplies

You will need plenty of electrical tape, staples, tie–wraps, and bridle rings during the cabling phase. These can be found at your local electrical supply house, where you can establish a line of credit for these items.

Conduit

We recommend flexible conduit with 2–inch OD (outside diameter) from Carlon, part number 12011, available in 500–foot reels. **www. carlon.com** The company has a host of accessories to splice, cap and support the conduit.

Run conduit from the electronics closet to the attic as a minimum for future system upgrades. If the home warrants it, then add additional runs of conduit to other service areas of the home, such as crawl spaces, and other access points for future upgrades.

Wallplate Mounting Brackets

Typical J-boxes are too shallow for volume controls, keypads, and infrared devices. We recommend low-voltage plastic plaster rings from Caddy. They have rings for both new work and old work in various sizes. See **www.caddy.com** for complete product details. Some installers use plastic boxes with the backs removed. While the NEC does not require sealed boxes for low voltage, you should check with your local code.

Caddy MP1S – Plate mounting bracket for new work. 25 per pack.

Caddy MP2S – Double gang plate mounting bracket for new work. 25 per pack

All measurements are ATF (above the finished floor), and are typically 12" to 18" from floor to top of box. Align boxes with the electrical outlets when possible. Check with the builder or supervisor for the dimensions of the flooring. Run all cables from the top of the box (plastic ring) and allow twelve (12) inches of cable to loop from the bottom.

Old Work Tools

Old work or retrofit as it is frequently called, requires a host of tools, and yes, a new set of skills. These tools and skills are out of the scope of this book. You can find many of the tools required at **www.lsdinc.com**

Termination Tools

Twisted Pair/Coax Termination Kit – The bulk of the work in the termination phase deals with termination of coaxial and twisted pair cables (cat5e). Ideal Industries makes a kit that suits the needs of this task very well. It includes products to cut, strip, terminate, and test cat5e, phone and coax. You can purchase this kit from your local distributor such as Graybar, see **www.graybar.com**. The kit consists of the following tools:

- Data T®–Cutter
- Scissors w/Stripping Notch
- Center Conductor Cutter
- UTP/Coax Stripper
- Coax Stripper w/Black Cassette
- Crimpmaster™ Frame Only
- 2,4,6–Position Die Set for RJ–11 Plugs
- 8–Position Die Set for RJ–45 Plugs
- RG–58/59/62 BNC Die Set
- Punchmaster™ II w/100 Blade
- Punchmaster™ II 66 Blade Only
- ABS™ Signal Thrower™
- ABS™ Tester
- ZipKit™ Carrying Case

Cable Testers

This is by far the most important part of the installation. You must test every cable and subsequently label each one. Below is a list of suggested test tools from Ideal Industries. You can find more about these products at **www.idealindustries.com**

Tone and Probe Kit – The amplifier probe and tone generator kit is designed to identify and trace cables within a group without damaging the insulators.

Butt Set – Ideal Industries ABS Tester (Almost a Butt Set) is a simple–to–use tester for basic troubleshooting of analog voice system installations. It monitors phone lines for dial tone quality and presence of power, tests for correct jack polarity (detects reversed tip and ring), and indicates call addressing for correct telephone extensions.

Unshielded 4 Pair UTP and Coaxial – Cable Tester. Ideal Industries makes a product, LinkMaster™ PRO Large Kit, which enables installers to map, test and troubleshoot data and voice communication cable and coax runs. It tests for shorts, opens, miswires, reversals, split pairs, and continuity. The product provides eight (8) termination tags that are placed in the cat5e jacks, and eight (8) CATV color–coded F–Terminators that are placed on the F terminations at the wallplates. In addition to mapping cables the tone mode generates four different tones on all pairs, a selected pair, or selected pin. In short you will use this tool every day.

Cables

Color Coding Your Cables

It is extremely important to give a separate color to each cable that has a different and distinct purpose.

- Color coding makes installation easy during the cabling phase. In the download we provide cabling stickers. We have created a sticker for each electronic device and listed the cables with specific colors so it is easy to figure out what cable to run where during the cabling phase.

- Bundle all similar color cables together in the equipment closet to make it easy to sort cables by function.

- When cables are terminated, use the same color for the cable and the termination connector. For example, White cat5e cables are terminated with white RJ45 connectors at both ends. This practice makes testing each cable run incredibly easy.

- Once the cables are terminated and tested, it is time to label them. This way it is easy to determine which cables have passed test. In other words, if the cable is labeled, it passed. If the cable is not labeled, it did not pass. This will save you countless hours of labeling and retesting cables.

More on cables...

- Wire is an electronic component of cable, referred to as the conductor. A cat5e cable has eight wires.
- Cable encases more than just the wire conductor.
- AWG stands for American Wire Gauge.
- The lower that the number on the gauge is, the thicker the wire.
- Wire ranges in sizes from 40 thru 1, 0, 00, 000, 0000.
- Solid core wire is typically used for strength, and stranded wire

is more flexible wire. So cat5e installed in the home behind the walls is solid and patch cords are stranded. If you make your own patch cords with the same cable used to run throughout the home they will not withstand the flexibility requirements of a patch cord and eventually will fail.

• Shielding keeps interference and noise from entering into the cable, and keeps signals from leaving a cable to help prevent interfering with adjacent cables. Always connect the shield to ground at the source end only. If connected at both ends the shield will become an antenna and increase the amount of interference.

Category Ratings

The category rating system was developed by the Telecommunications Industry Associations (TIA) in response to industry demands for higher data rate specifications on application over unshielded twisted pair (UTP).

Rating	Bandwidth	Typical Application
cat3	16 MHz	Voice, ISDN, 4 Mbps Token Ring and 10Base–T
cat4	20 MHz	Same as Cat3
cat5	100 MHz	Voice and Data, being replaced by cat5e.
cat5e	350 MHz	This is the recommended cable for today's voice and data systems. Use this cable for all of your voice and data requirements.
cat6	500 MHz	Gigabits, new technology, consider using in the near future.

Figure 4.4
UTP Cable
Ratings

Jacket Materials

PVC (Polyvinyl Chloride) – Most common type of cable jacketing used in residential wiring. The temperature rating is –55C (minus 55 degrees Centigrade) to 105C (One hundred five degrees Centigrade). The cable jacket is smooth and pliable.

Teflon – Used in plenum (air handling area) situations. The temperature rating is much higher at 260C (two hundred sixty degrees Centigrade). Rarely used in residential applications.

Rubber – Material has excellent durability and flexibility. It is primarily used for out–of–wall applications, (i.e. as a finish cable for the short distance between a speaker jack and the speaker). Rubber is not rated for in–wall usage

Cable Identifiers

Cable Identifier	NEC Article	Environmental Rating
CL2X	725, Class 2	Residential
CL2		Commercial
CL2R		Riser
CL2P		Plenum
CL3X	725, Class 3	Residential
CL3		Commercial
CL3R		Riser
CL3P		Plenum
PLTC	725, Class 3, Outdoor	Commercial
CMX	800, Communications	Residential
CM		Commercial
CMR		Riser
CMP		Plenum
CATVX	820, CATV	Residential
CATV		Commercial
CATVR		Riser

Figure 4.5
Cable
Identifiers

Environmental Ratings

The following designations are defined by the Nartional Electrical Code (NEC).

Residential – Cables in one– and two–family dwellings must pass *VW–1 Vertical Wire Flame Test*, which is the least stringent flame test.

Commercial – Any non–residential installation not characterized by Plenum or Riser (explained below). Cable must pass *UL–1558 Vertical Flame Tray test*.

Plenum – Cable is installed in air handling areas where smoke or flames from a burning cable could spread rapidly in the airduct (Plenum). Cable must pass *UL–910 Modified Stiener Tunnel test*.

Riser – Cable is used in non–air handling areas such as elevators or other vertical shafts. Cable must pass *UL–1666 Vertical Riser Flame test*.

Articles from the NEC Code

725 – Covers remote control, signaling and power–limited circuits that are not part of a device or appliance. Includes HVAC, sprinklers, fire & burglar alarms, music systems and computer networks.

800 – Covers communications circuits. Includes telephone.

820 – Covers community antenna television (CATV) systems. Includes television and other signals over coaxial cables.

Recommended Cables

We have included a list of recommend cables, their colors and purposes. Sticking to this standard will save countless hours of toning
and testing your cables. We cannot stress enough how important
this is to ensuring a successful installation.

cat5e–WH – Telephone. All cables are run from the wallplate to
the telephone panel.

AWG (gauge)	24	Jacket Color	White
Pairs	4	Jacket Material	PVC
Conductors	8	NEC Identifier	CL3X
Conductor Type	Solid	Shield	None

cat5e–BL – Home Networking. All cables are run from the wallplate to the networking panel

AWG (gauge)	24	Jacket Color	Blue
Pairs	4	Jacket Material	PVC
Conductors	8	NEC Identifier	CL3X
Conductor Type	Solid	Shield	None

cat5e–YL – Keypads. All cables are run from the keypad or wallplate to the integrated system.

AWG (gauge)	24	Jacket Color	Yellow
Pairs	4	Jacket Material	PVC
Conductors	8	NEC Identifier	CL3X
Conductor Type	Solid	Shield	None

cat5e–PK – Music Input and Music Output Wallplates. All cables
are run from the wallplate to the whole–home music rack.

AWG (gauge)	24	Jacket Color	Pink
Pairs	4	Jacket Material	PVC
Conductors	8	NEC Identifier	CL3X
Conductor Type	Solid	Shield	None

cat5e–GY – Integrated Controls, such as lighting, HVAC, and security. All cables are run to the integrated system.

AWG (gauge)	24	Jacket Color	Gray
Pairs	4	Jacket Material	PVC
Conductors	8	NEC Identifier	CL3X
Conductor Type	Solid	Shield	None

cat5e–GR – Thermostats – All cables are run from the wallplate to the thermostat panel.

AWG (gauge)	24	Jacket Color	Green
Pairs	4	Jacket Material	PVC
Conductors	8	NEC Identifier	CL3X
Conductor Type	Solid	Shield	None

RG6QD–BK – CATV. All cables are run from the wallplate to the televi–sion panel.

AWG (gauge)	18	Jacket Color	Black
Pairs		Jacket Material	PVC
Conductors	1	NEC Identifier	CL3X
Conductor Type	Solid	Shield	2 foil, 2 brade

RG6QD–WH – Satellite, FM Radio, and XM Radio – All cables are run from the wallplate or antenna locations to the satellite panel.

AWG (gauge)	18	Jacket Color	White
Pairs		Jacket Material	PVC
Conductors	1	NEC Identifier	CL3X
Conductor Type	Solid	Shield	2 foil, 2 brade

90

IR20/4–BK – Infrared Controls. All cables are run from the infrared receiver to the infrared connection block, typically located in the home theater equipment rack.

AWG (gauge)	20	Jacket Color	Black
Pairs	2	Jacket Material	PVC
Conductors	4	NEC Identifier	CL3X
Conductor Type	Stranded	Shield	Foil

S14/4–BL – Speakers from system to keypad/volume control. All cables are run from the keypad or volume control to the whole home music rack. Select cable gauge based on the following dis–tances.

- 16 gauge – up to 100 ft.
- 14 gauge – up to 175 ft.
- 12 gauge – beyond 175 ft.

AWG (gauge)	14	Jacket Color	Blue
Pairs		Jacket Material	PVC
Conductors	4	NEC Identifier	CL3X
Conductor Type	Stranded	Shield	None

S16/2–WH – Speakers from keypad/volume control to speakers. All cables are run from the speaker to keypad or volume control location.

AWG (gauge)	16	Jacket Color	White
Pairs		Jacket Material	PVC
Conductors	2	NEC Identifier	CL3X
Conductor Type	Stranded	Shield	None

Telephone Jack Connections

Figure 3.6 shows the pinout for all telephone jack connections. It is the standard called for in the TIA/EIA–570–A Residential Telecommunications Cabling Standard. Figure 3.7 shows type typical pin usage for an analog telephone system. In this application pair 1 (pins 4,5) carry the telephone line, and pair 2 (pins 3,6) carry power to the telephone. In a digital phone system a single pair (pins 4,5) carry both power and a digital phone line. For a plain old telephone pair 1 and pair 2 will carry line 1 and line 2 respectively.

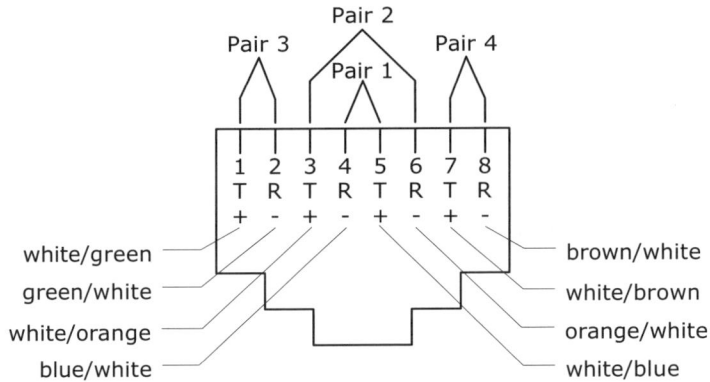

Figure 4.6
T568A
Pinout

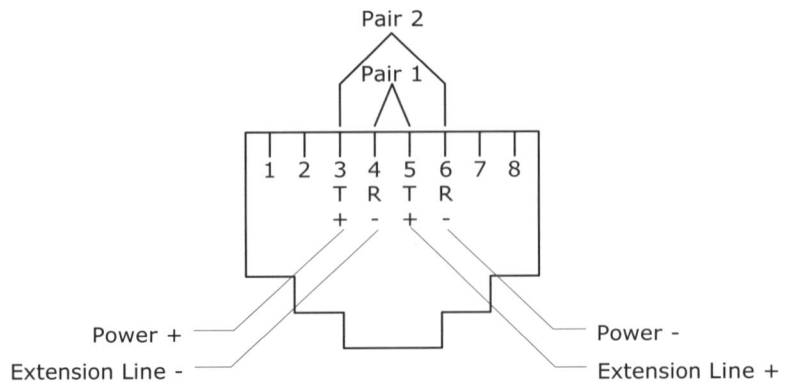

white/green —
green/white —
white/orange —
blue/white —
brown/white
white/brown
orange/white
white/blue

Figure 4.7
Analog Telphone
System Pinout

Power +
Extension Line -
Power -
Extension Line +

Network Jack Connections

Figure 3.8 shows the pinout for all networking jack connections. T568A is supposed to be the standard for new installations, however, most off–the–shelf data equipment and cables are wired to T568B. In fact very few people use T568A to wire their network. It's important not to mix systems, as both you and your equipment will become hopelessly confused. Figure 3.9 shows the pinout configuration of 10BaseT or Ethernet. The pinout is for the NIC (network interface connector) side of the cable. While both sides of the patch cable are connected via T568B, the hub side will have the transmit and receive connections reversed. The cable length between the NIC and hub should not exceed 325ft, which includes the cables in the wall and all patch cords.

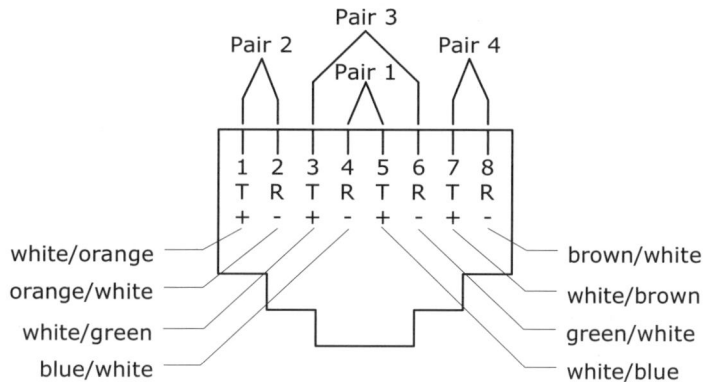

Figure 4.8
T568B
Pinout

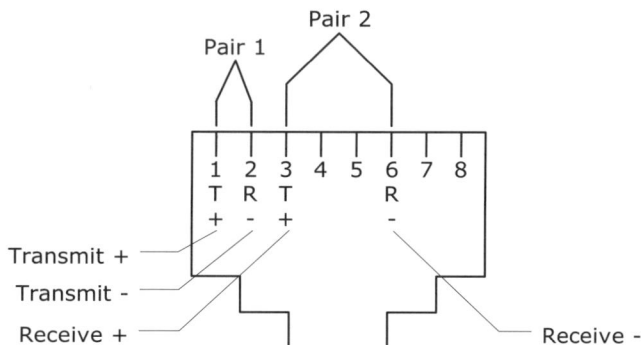

Pair 3
Pair 2   Pair 1   Pair 4

1	2	3	4	5	6	7	8
T	R	T	R	T	R	T	R
+	-	+	-	+	-	+	-

white/orange — brown/white
orange/white — white/brown
white/green — green/white
blue/white — white/blue

Figure 4.9
10BaseT
Pinout

Pair 2
Pair 1

1	2	3	4	5	6	7	8
T	R	T			R		
+	-	+			-		

Transmit +
Transmit -
Receive +
Receive -

93

Telephone & Networking WP

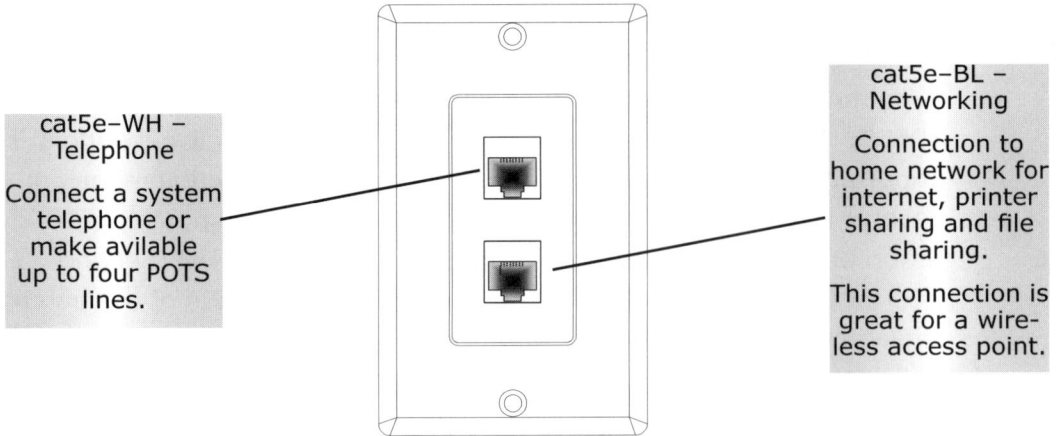

cat5e–WH –
Telephone

Connect a system
telephone or
make avilable
up to four POTS
lines.

cat5e–BL –
Networking

Connection to
home network for
internet, printer
sharing and file
sharing.

This connection is
great for a wire-
less access point.

Purpose

The telephone & networking wallplate provides access for four (4)
telephone lines and a home networking connection.

Cabling

- cat5e–BL, cat5e–WH
- Install bracket at the same height
as the electrician's outlet box.
- Run cables from distribution panels to wallplate.
- Run all cables from top of the
mounting bracket and allow the
cable to extend past the bottom by
twelve (12) inches.

Termination

- Telephone – Punch down white
cat5e jacks at both the wallplate and
the distribution panels, terminate on
white cat5e cable according to the
T568A standard.
- Networking – Punch down blue
cat5e jacks at the distribution panel
and white cat5e jacks at the wallplate, terminate on blue cat5e cable
according to the T586B standard.
- Test all cables and label cables that
pass.
- Place a plastic bag over connections at the wallplate and stuff back
into the wall.

Move–In

- Attach a wallplate to mounting
bracket, make sure it is level, then
clean both the wallplate and the area
around it.

94

Multimedia Wallplate

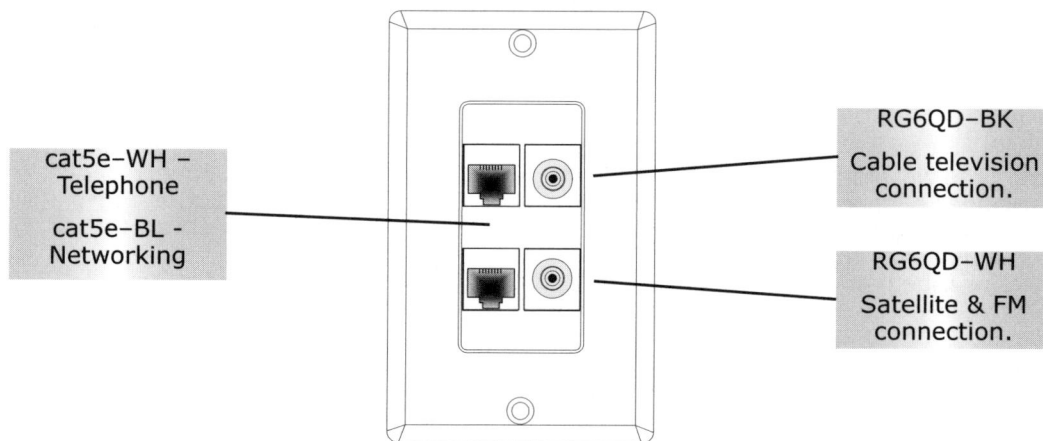

cat5e–WH –
Telephone

cat5e–BL -
Networking

RG6QD–BK

Cable television
connection.

RG6QD–WH

Satellite & FM
connection.

Purpose

The multimedia wallplate provides access for cable television, satellite, four (4) telephone lines, and a home networking connection.

Cabling

• RG6QD–BK,RG6QD–WH, Cat5–BL, Cat5–WH
• Install mounting bracket at the same height as the electrician's box.
• Run cables from the distribution panels to the wallplate.
• Run all cables from the top of the mounting bracket and allow the cable to extend past the bottom by twelve (12) inches.

Termination

• Telephone – Punch down white cat5e jacks at both the wallplate and the distribution panels, terminate on white cat5e cable according to the T568A standard.
• Networking – Punch down blue cat5e jacks at the distribution panel and white cat5e jacks at the wallplate, terminate on blue cat5e cable according to the T586B standard.
• CATV & Satellite – Use Compression fit connectors at both the wallplate and distribution panels.
• Test all cables and label cables that pass.
• Place a plastic bag over connections at the wallplate and stuff back into the wall.

Move–In

• Attach the wallplate to mounting bracket, make sure it is level, and then clean both the wallplate and the area around it.

95

Surround–Sound Wall Plate

L&R speaker connection to the surround speakers. The wallplate includes a 14/4 speaker cable from the music system, leave it behind this wallplate. To convert surround speakers to music speakers tie surround speakers to the 14/4.

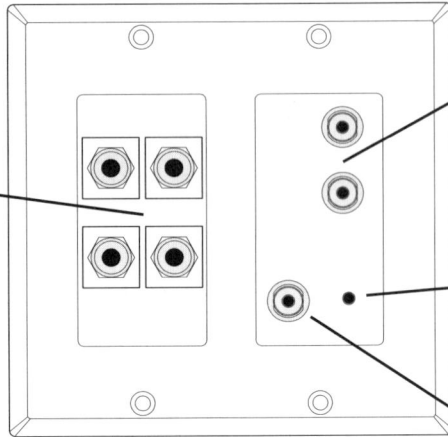

L&R Audio from Music System. A zone is dedicated to this system, sent full volume. Connect to AUX input on Surround processor.

IR Connection – Sends infrafred signals from integrated control system

This section of the wallplate is the Elan IRWAP. This connection is unused.

2x – RG6QD–BK CATV – used to connect to both the television and the VCR

2x – RG6QD–WH Satellite – used to connect to two feeds for Tivo based reciever.

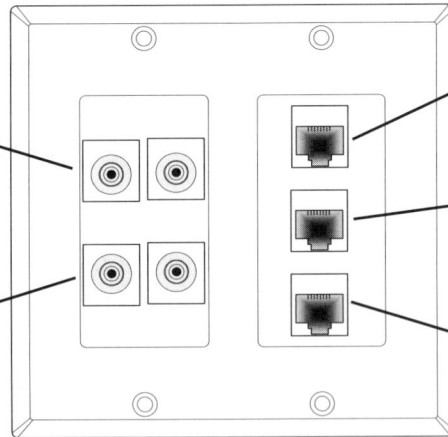

cat5e–GY ICS Network – used to tie into the integrated control system.

cat5e–WH Telephone – connect to satellite.

cat5e–BL Networking – connection for home networking for devices such as Tivo, and some IP based receivers.

Purpose

The surround sound wallplate provides two (2) connections for cable television; two (2) connections for satellite, four (4) telephone lines, and connections to a home network, the home–wide stereo, the home–wide integration system, and cabling for surround sound speakers.

Cabling

- (2)RG6QD–BK,(2)RG6QD–WH, cat5e–BL, cat5e–WH, cat5e–GY, cat5e–GR, 14/4–BL, 16/2–WH to surrounds
- Install (2) two–gang mounting brackets at the same height as the electrician's box.
- Run cables from the distribution panels to the wallplate.
- Run all cables from the top of the mounting bracket and allow the cable to extend past the bottom by twelve (12) inches.

Termination

- Telephone – Punch down white cat5e jacks at both the wallplate and the distribution panels, terminate on white cat5e cable according to the T568A standard.
- Networking – Punch down blue cat5e jacks at the distribution panel and white cat5e jacks at the wallplate, terminate on blue cat5e cable according to the T586B standard.
- Integrated Control System Network (ICS) – Punch down blue cat5e jacks at the distribution panel and white cat5e jacks at the wallplate, terminate on Grey cat5e cable according to the T586B standard.
- Home–Wide Stereo – Using the pink cat5e cable, install the Elan IRWAP (balanced line driver) per the manufactures instructions. Place the plate label "System" at the wallplate location, and the "Source" at the distribtuion panel location.
- Surround Speakers – Terminate the white 16/2 speaker cable to the binding posts at the wallplates and connect to the surround speakers.
- CATV & Satellite – Use Compression fit connectors at both the wallplate and distribution panels.
- Test all cables and label cables that pass.
- Place a plastic bag over connections at the wallplate and stuff back into the wall.

Move–In

- Attach a wallplate to mounting bracket, make sure it is level, then clean both the wallplate and the area around it.

Music & Video Output Wallplate

This is the Elan IRWAP. It converts unbalanced audio to balanced so it can be sent over a Cat5e–PK cable.

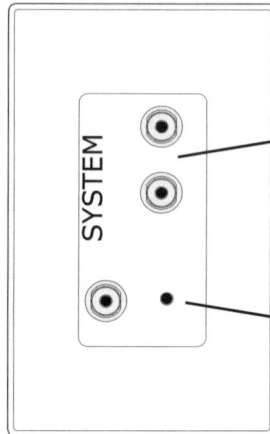

SYSTEM

L&R Audio from Music System. A zone is dedicated to this location, sent full volume. Connect to AUX input on Surround processor.

IR Connection – Sends infra-red signals from integrated control system

Purpose

The music & video output wallplate sends a signal from the main entertainment center to a music or video consumer electronic device. This is typically installed as part of the surround–sound wallplate to send music from the central music system to the surround receiver located at the wallplate.

Cabling

• (2) cat5e–PK – The second cable is used for long runs to prevent too much signal loss.
• For composite video distribution install a set of "Balun" modules such as Russound's MOD–VB.
• Install mounting bracket at the same height as the electrician's box.
• Run cables from the distribution panels to the wallplate.

• Run all cables from the top of the mounting bracket and allow the cable to extend past the bottom by twelve (12) inches.

Termination

• Home–Wide Stereo – Using the pink cat5e cable, install the Elan IRWAP (balanced line driver) per the manufactures instructions. Place the plate label "System" at the wallplate location, and the "Source" at the distribtuion panel location.
• Test all cables and label cables that pass.
• Place a plastic bag over connections at the wallplate and stuff back into the wall.

Move–In

• Attach the wallplate to mounting bracket, make sure it is level, and then clean both the wallplate and the area around it.

98

Music & Video Input Wallplate

This is the Elan IRWAP. It converts unbalanced audio to balanced so it can be sent over a Cat5e–PK cable.

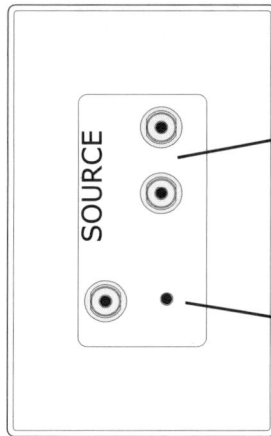

SOURCE

L&R Audio from this location are sent to the music system. Use this to remotely locate the CD player and other audio devices.

IR Connection – connects the emitter here to allow music system to control the local device.

Purpose

The music & video input wallplate sends a music and video signal from a consumer electronic device to the main entertainment center. This is typically used to remotely locate a CD player in the home that is source for the home–wide music system.

Cabling

• (2) cat5e–PK – The second cable is used for long runs to prevent too much signal loss.
• For composite video distribution install a set of "Balun" modules such as Russound's MOD–VB.
• Install mounting bracket at the same height as the electrician's box.
• Run cables from the distribution panels to the wallplate.
• Run all cables from the top of the mounting bracket and allow the cable to extend past the bottom by twelve (12) inches.

Termination

• Home–Wide Stereo – Using the pink cat5e cable, install the Elan IRWAP (balanced line driver) per the manufactures instructions. Place the plate label "Source" at the wallplate location, and the "System" at the distribtuion panel location.
• Test all cables and label cables that pass.
• Place a plastic bag over connections at the wallplate and stuff back into the wall.

Move–In

• Attach the wallplate to mounting bracket, make sure it is level, and then clean both the wallplate and the area around it.

Telephone & Home Networking Panel

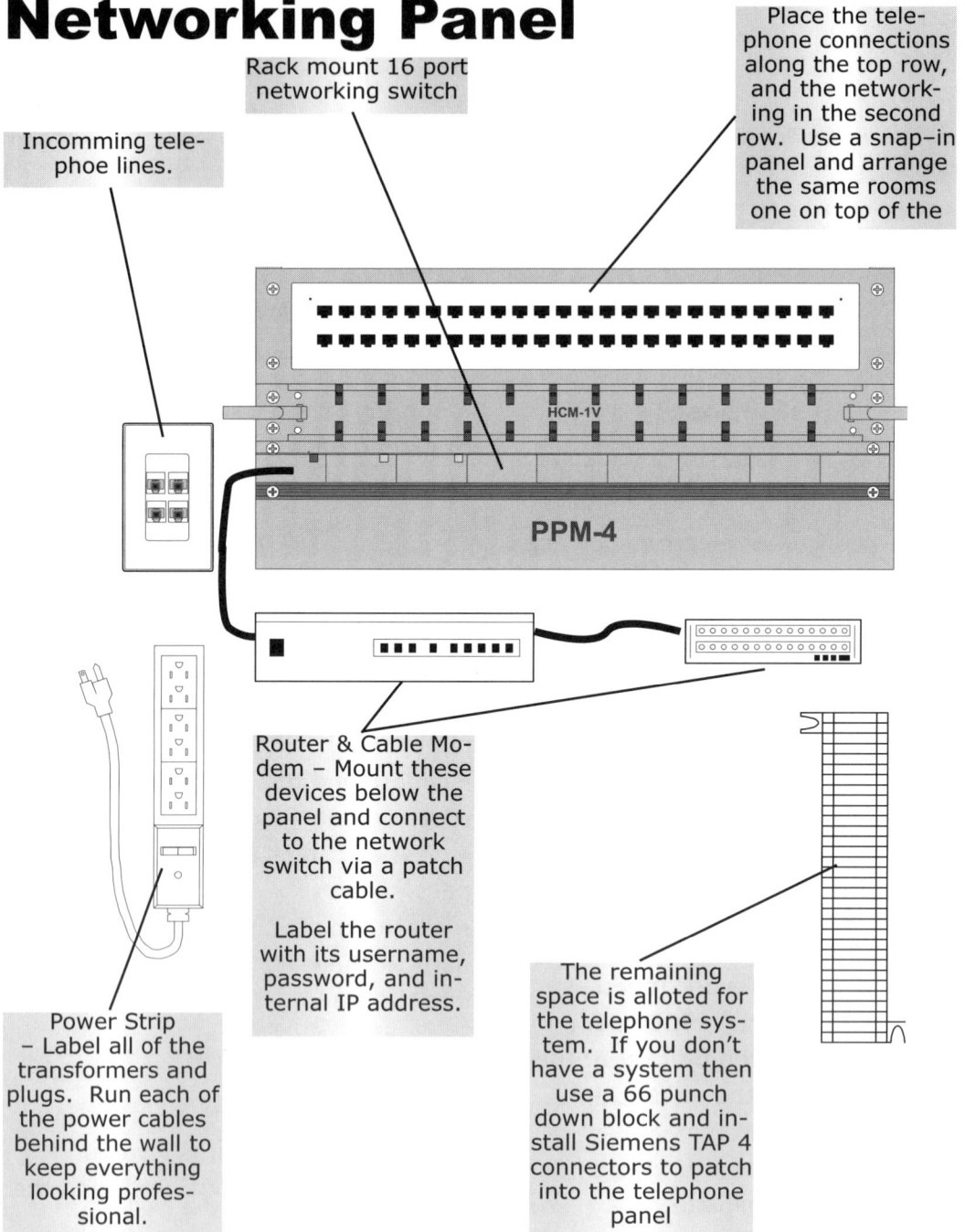

Rack mount 16 port networking switch

Place the telephone connections along the top row, and the networking in the second row. Use a snap–in panel and arrange the same rooms one on top of the

Incomming tele-phoe lines.

HCM-1V

PPM-4

Router & Cable Mo-dem – Mount these devices below the panel and connect to the network switch via a patch cable.

Label the router with its username, password, and in-ternal IP address.

Power Strip – Label all of the transformers and plugs. Run each of the power cables behind the wall to keep everything looking profes-sional.

The remaining space is alloted for the telephone sys-tem. If you don't have a system then use a 66 punch down block and in-stall Siemens TAP 4 connectors to patch into the telephone panel

100

Purpose

The telephone & home networking distribution panel is designed to provide an easy connection between the telephone system, home networking switches, routers, and the wallplates.

Cabling

- Run all of the telephone, white cat5e cables to this panel.
- Run all of the networking, blue cat5e cables to this panel.
- Drill a 2" hole centered on the panel and extend all of the cables 36" beyond the plywood panel.

Termination

- Use white cat5e jacks to terminate the telephone cat5e white cables according to the T586A standard.
- Use white cat5e jacks to terminate the telephone cat5e white cables according to the T586B standard.
- After each wallplate has been terminated test each connection.
- As each cable passes test, label that cable with the name of the room where the wallplate is located.

Service Connections

The telephone service connections wallplate provides access to four (4) incoming telephone lines at the telephone distribution panel.

Cabling

- Install mounting bracket just below the telephone and networking panel, leaving space to the right (18"width x 12" height) for the telephone system. Use a surface mounted metal one–gang open back electrical box for mounting.
- Run cables from the telephone service provider's Telco box to the wallplate.
- Drill a ¾" hole and bring the cable 12" to 18" beyond the panel.

Termination

- Use white cat5e jacks at the wallplate, and terminate according to the T586B standard.
- Connect the cables as shown in the table above.
- Use a linesman telephone to test each incoming phone line. If you call your cell number from each line you can test the number with your caller ID.

Cable Television panel

Leviton Multimedia Panel

This box (14w x 24h x 6d) comes with a cover to create a professional look and house all of the cable connections.

2" hole allows cable to be routed behind the plywood wall.

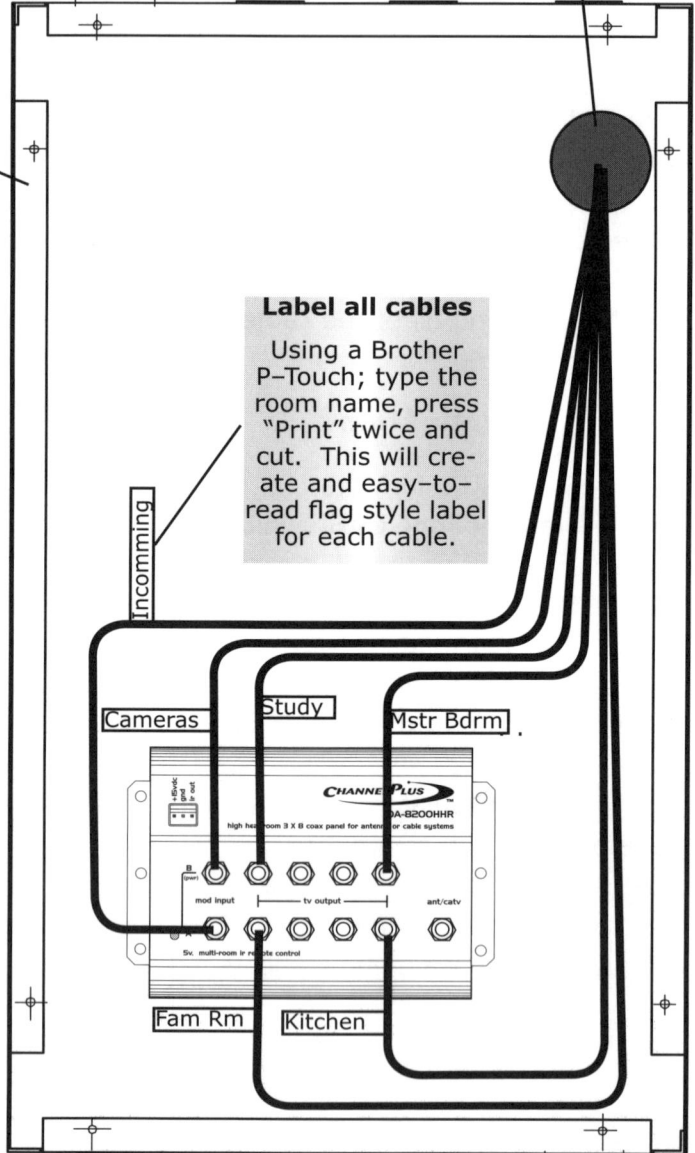

Label all cables

Using a Brother P–Touch; type the room name, press "Print" twice and cut. This will create and easy–to–read flag style label for each cable.

Power Strip – Label all of the transformers and plugs. Run each of the power cables behind the wall to keep everything looking professional.

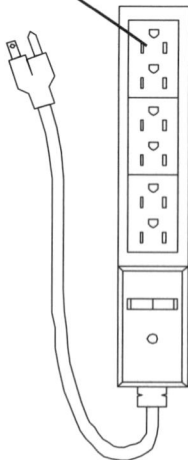

Incoming

Cameras

Study

Mstr Bdrm

CHANNEL PLUS

DA-8200HHR

high headroom 3 X 8 coax panel for antenna or cable systems

mod input

tv output

ant/catv

5v. multi-room ir remote control

Fam Rm

Kitchen

Purpose

Based on a Channel Plus 8200 amplifier with an integrated infrared (IR) engine, the cable television panel provides amplification to drive all of the televisions in the home. It also allows the IR engine to control and modulate the remote equipment. In other words, your customer will be able to operate a DVD player, satellite receiver or any other audio/video device from a central location and from every television in the home.

Cabling

• Run all of the television, black RG6QD cables to this panel.
• Drill a 2" hole in the upper right corner of the panel and extend all of the cables 36" beyond the plywood panel.

Termination

• Use snap–and–seal connectors on each cable.
• After each wallplate has been terminated test each connection.
• As each cable passes test, label that cable with the name of the room where the wallplate is located.

Service Connections

The television service connection runs from a ground block on the incomming cable signal to the input on the radio frequency (RF) amplifier.

High Definition Digital Satellite Panel

Leviton Multimedia Panel

This box (14w x 24h x 6d) comes with a cover to create a professional look and house all of the cable connections.

2" hole allows cable to be routed behind the plywood wall.

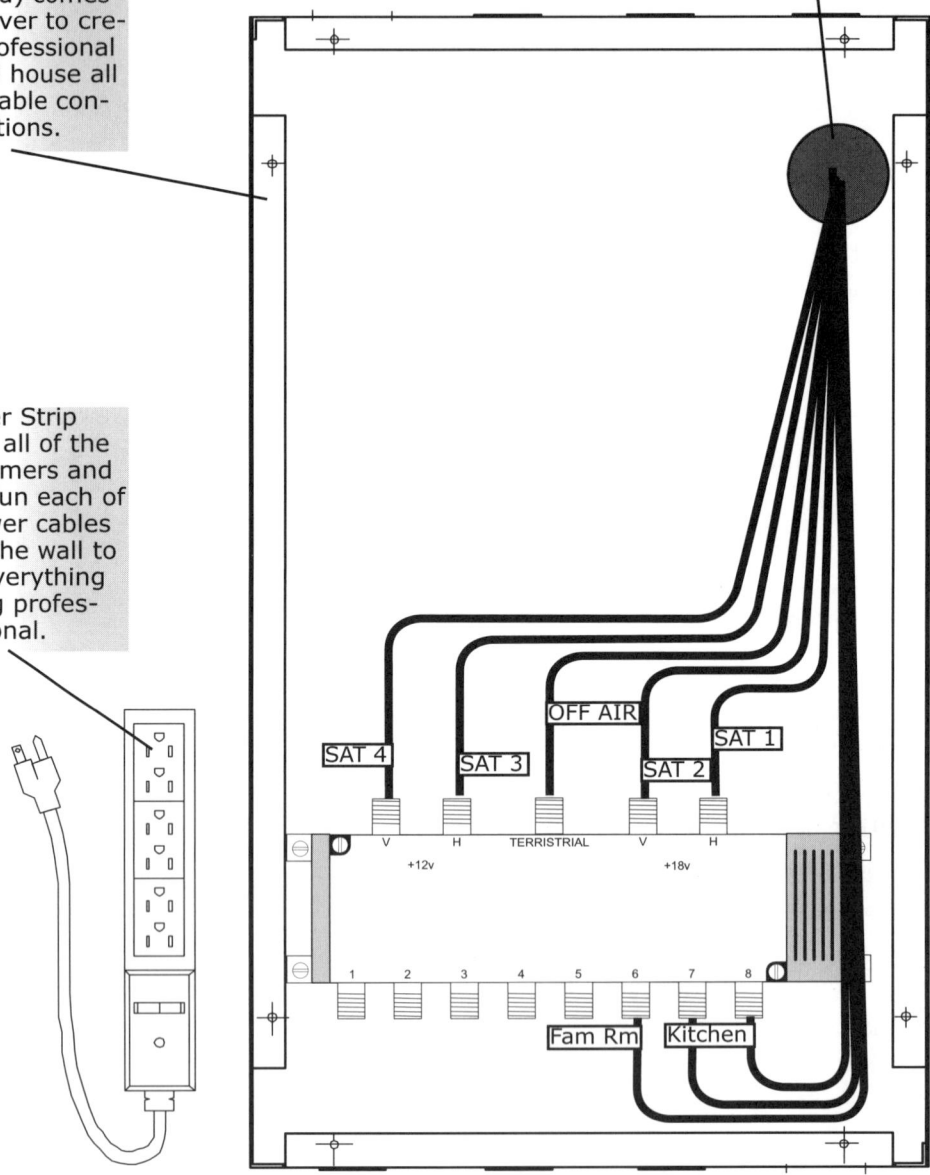

Power Strip – Label all of the transformers and plugs. Run each of the power cables behind the wall to keep everything looking professional.

SAT 4

SAT 3

OFF AIR

SAT 2

SAT 1

V   H   TERRISTRIAL   V   H

+12v   +18v

1   2   3   4   5   6   7   8

Fam Rm   Kitchen

The high definition digital satellite panel includes a 21–inch dish and a Spaun multiswitch that takes the high definition satellite signal and distributes it throughout your home.

Service Connections

• Run five (5) white RG6 quad shielded cables from the attic to the satellite distribution panel, usually in the basement. In addition, run a #10 ground cable to the same location. Leave an extra twenty–five (25) feet of both cables in the attic to allow for placement of the satellite dish. Note: terminate the shielded cables along with the ground cable to the grounding block in the basement. From the grounding block, run the cables outside the home to the satellite dish.
• Bundle the cables at the satellite distribution panel in the basement and label "Sat feed".

Grounding the Dish

There must be an earth ground of antennae before the system enters the structure. This earth ground should be a tie to the ground rod at the service entrance. NEC article 250 explains in detail the code for grounding all electrical devices.

Pointing the Dish

With DSS receiver dishes, the dish must be pointed towards the south when installing a dish in the Northern Hemisphere. In the U.S. this means also pointing the dish somewhere towards the south and towards the middle of the U.S.

Off–Air High Definition Television and FM Antenna

The off–air high definition television and FM upgrade includes a digital antenna for off–air HDTV and FM reception. Reception depends on the location of the home, and actual channels will vary.

Antenna Installation

• Follow manufacturer's specifications and local code.
• Tie the antenna to the earth ground before you bring the system to the structure.
• Tie the antenna to ground rod at service entrance.

Steps to Installing a Structured Wiring System

We're going to divide the structured wiring system into three unique phases: the cabling phase, the termination phase, and the move–in phase.

How Much Time?

To determine how much time you will need for the cabling phase, you can think of it in terms of 16–hour increments. That means two guys a day. A typical cabling phase will be anywhere from 64 to 128 hours of labor. The termination phase will usually represent about half as much time as required by the cabling phase. In other words, if you bid 64 hours of cabling labor, then plan on roughly 32 hours of termination labor. The move–in phase will represent half again as much of that time, so you will need 16 hours of labor for the move–in phase.

Figure 4.10 shows an estimate of required cabling time based upon the house size, wallplates, speakers, keypads and thermostats in the home. Typically larger homes will require more devices, the cable runs will be longer, thus increasing the time required.

Time (Hours)	House Size	Wall-plates	Speaker Pairs	Keypads	Thermo-stats
96	5,000	12	8	8	4
128	7,500	18	12	14	6
160	10,000	24	16	20	8
256	15,000	32	24	28	12

Figure 4.10 Estimated Cabling Hours

Cabling Phase – Stickers

Multimedia Wallplate

Cat–5e BLUE & WHITE

RG6–QD BLACK & WHITE

MP1S mounting bracket
at outlet height

Your Company Name Here!
123 Main Street, Anytown, MA 01234
(999) 555 – 1234

Figure 4.11
Cabling
Sticker

The first step in the cabling phase is placing cabling stickers throughout the home. A sample of a sticker is shown in figure 4.11. This book's download includes sticker templates for every device. The stickers mark the locations of all the wallplates, keypads and touchscreens throughout the home. For example, a customer may want a telephone wallplate in the kitchen. We have included a Wallplate Location Table with our Customer Information Sheets. The table indicates what type and where (which rooms) the customer wants the wallplates installed.

Take the stickers to the home and stick them to the studs in the locations where the wallplates will be installed. The sales person is typically assigned this responsibility. However, sometimes it is the role of the project manager. It depends on the division of responsibilities between sales and project management, and the needs of your customer. It is a good practice to write the room name in the door jam framing.

Once all the stickers are in place, it's a good opportunity to record any changes on the Customer Information Table. Frequently what happens is the sales person will "sticker" the home by him or herself, and reviews it later with the customer. Or the sales person places these stickers in the home along with the customer. In this case, the customer refers to the builder, the architect, the owner, and sometimes all three. On many occasions the customer will request extra locations while performing the sticker walkthrough.

Now that your personnel have "stickered" the home, there should be bright yellow, or other fluorescent colored stickers on the walls throughout the home. This makes it easy for the installation team to come in and run the cabling. Theoretically, the installation team needs zero documentation – beyond the customer's address. The team can come into the site with the standard tools and standard cabling, and install the cabling with little to no discussion with the sales person or project manager.

However, every now and again there is a reason to discuss a home that has some peculiarities to it, or if you need to do things outside of your normal standard. This could include something like the satellite dish must be cabled to a crawl space, rather than to an open attic.

Placing the stickers throughout the home is the most critical step in cabling phase. Do not start a job until you get the home fully "stickered". Do not start a job until you get your customer OK on the locations of the "stickers".

On occasions you'll run into a situation where you can only "sticker" the first and second floors, and then come back another time to "sticker" the basement. That's OK, but make sure you get the major chunks of the work done at one time. If you know that's going to be the case, that you're going to have to come back multiple times, then make sure that you build in extra labor time in your bid estimate. Every time you go back you can be sure the labor will go up more than just incrementally.

You can purchse laser printable permanent adhesive shipping labels in a multitude of flourescent colors from **www.uline.com**. We recommend the 4" x 3 1/3" labels with 6 labels per sheet.

Wallplate Location Table Update

The information on Wallplate Location Table should now be updated to reflect the changes during the sticker process. Then the table can be used as a work order to hand off to the installers. The Wallplate Location Table (figure 4.1) specifies all the wallplates, and distribution panel configurations.

Cabling the Home

The next step is the actual installation of the cables. Cables from the second floor should be drilled up to the attic, and then bundled together into a main trunk. And then from there at one or two locations, depending on the size of the home, run the trunk to the distribution panels, located in the electronics closet in the basement.

This allows you to go into the attic when the job is completed and snake cables in for old work. It also allows you to repair cables and to have access to those cables for maintenance and possible expansion work in the future.

From the first floor, drill your holes down to the basement. Then make a large trunk, keeping the low–voltage cables away from electrical cables, of course. There is a whole list of Best Practices to help you when it comes to cabling.

After the cables are in place, the next step is to put in a distribution panel wall. Sometimes the builder will do this, however sometimes it's just as easy to bring in your own plywood and framing lumber.

The best way to construct a distribution panel is to build a wall using 2x4s and 3/4–inch plywood. Attach the plywood on top of the 2x4s. We recommend at least one sheet of plywood and in larger jobs, two sheets, or perhaps even more. Think about how much space is required for each one of the distribution panels and then lay it out on the plywood wall appropriately.

We've given you some basic dimensions in this chapter on the sizes of distribution panels. It's important to get this work completed in the cabling phase to get prepared for the termination phase. Keep the wall away from the cement foundation by a couple of inches, so that you can work with the cables behind the walls. Then go ahead and lay out your distribution panels. This doesn't mean install them. Rather it means mark in pencil where the panels are going to go, and drill the appropriate size holes, which typically are 1 1/2- to 2-inch holes and bring all your cables through keeping all one color cables together.

Remember that so far none of your cables are labeled. At this point, you can cut all your cables to length. Leave six feet for distribution panels, and twelve feet for cables going to the equipment rack. Bundle all cables neatly and put tape around them. This looks very professional, and will build confidence in your team's ability to deliver.

Cabling Quality Check

The last step in the cabling phase is to check the work. The original sales person or the project manager (if the responsibility was turned over to him/her.) is assigned the task to ensure the work is complete and professional. Take a look at the job; check to see whether all the requirements have been met; and make sure everything is clean, neat and no trash has been left behind. The result is a very professional looking job. At this point the project manager should send out the "Completion of Cabling" letter to the customer, thus notifying him/her of the completed work and allowing the customer to review the work before the next phase.

Cabling – When Should It Happen?

The cabling phase is started when all the other subcontractors are finished with their jobs. This will put a lot of pressure on you because many builders won't have set aside the time for you to come in and complete your work. You have to be very insistent and firm with the builder about the amount of time that's required to get your job completed. Do not under estimate the time you will need. It is best to over estimate your labor time. Let the builder know that you can't get your work finished until the plumber, the electrician and the HVAC contractors have completed their work.

Yes, it's going to slow down the building process, but that's the appropriate sequence in the building process. However many builders are not acquainted with the low–voltage step in the building process, and will try to squeeze you and convince you to start your project while other contractors are still in the home. In other words, it will take you a lot longer to get the work completed because you'll end up redoing work, and it probably won't come out neat and clean.

Termination – Overview

Now you are ready for the next step. Your plywood wall is up; your cables are run through it by color; and they are ready to be terminated. The next crew can come in as soon as the following day, and terminate the cables – even before the drywall goes up. Or they can come in as late as a few days prior to the customer move–in day. This allows you some slack in scheduling the next crew. If times are lean and you don't have enough work, you can accelerate your termination schedule by scheduling the termination closer and closer to the completion of the cabling phase. The opposite is also true. If you are heavy on work, you can delay your termination and push it out all the way to a few days before your customer moves in. It's a good way to be able to reduce and expand your labor force by being able to move the termination phase forward or backward in time. If you decide to terminate the cables prior to the installation of drywall you should wait for drywall before testing.

During the termination phase you will take those cables you installed during the cabling phase, terminate them at both ends, test them, label them, make the distribution panels and do the preparatory work required to bring services into the home. Services could include satellite, telephone, television, networking, cable and any other source your customer has selected.

The Distribution Panels

The first two steps in the termination phase are building your distribution panels and terminating the cables. Typically, a termination crew consists of two people. Instruct one person to build your distribution panels in the basement; and instruct the other person to terminate the wallplates throughout the home. All the terminated cables and wallplates should be left hanging from the wall. At the same time, you have to keep in mind there are other contractors working around the home (even though the ideal would be that you were the only contractor on the premises). That means the crew won't be able to leave the cables and wallplates hanging indefinitely, but they can be left hanging for that day.

Your crew should spend the better part of the day terminating the cables in the basement and upstairs. Toward the end of the day, it's time to break out the test tools and walkie-talkies and test the cables.

The Wallplates

We have included termination instructions for each wallplate in this chapter. You can terminate the wallplate as soon as the drywall is installed and as late as the day before move-in. This will give you an opportunity to schedule the work based upon your company's workload.

Place plastic bags over the terminations after testing the cables. This will preserve the connectors throughout the project.

Test and Label

A typical test on a coaxial cable goes like this:

- One person puts an identifier on a wallplate. The other person is downstairs in the basement at the distribution panel with the coax test gear.
- When that person gets a positive read on the cable, he/she will call upstairs, on the walkie–talkie, and say, "I got the blue identifier to pass."
- The upstairs person calls back to the person in the basement and says, "I'm in the living room."
- This tells the person in the basement to take the label that's marked 'living room" and attach it to that cable in the basement.
- When the basement person attaches the label marked living room, it also signifies that the cable has passed test.
- Now the person upstairs takes the identifier off the coaxial cable, and goes to the next wallplate for the next test.

You can use this same process with the RJ 45 speaker cables. We also recommend you build a small test tool to simplify testing the speaker cables. After you put banana jacks on the basement end, you can go to the volume control location and plug in the cables on your test tool.

When everything is terminated, tested and labeled, take the ends of all your terminated cables and put them in little plastic bags. Many connectors that you use to terminate are sold in small plastic bags. Put each of the connectors at the wallplate end back in the plastic bag, and stuff them back into the wall.

Preparing for the Equipment Rack

The equipment rack houses the music system and the integrated control system. When built properly it will have quick disconnects for each of the services required, such as telephone, television, and networking.

Install the following cables and terminate as specified for the particular cable.

- Run two white coaxial cables (RG6–WH) from the satellite panel.
- Run one black coaxial cable (RG6–BK) from the CATV panel.
- Run one white catagory 5e cable (cat5e–WH) from the telephone panel.
- Run one blue category 5e cable (cat5e–BL) from the networking panel
- Run one gray category 5e cable(cat5e–GY) from the security system
- Run one gray category 5e cable(cat5e–GY) from the HVAC system
- Run one gray category 5e cable(cat5e–GY) from the lighting system

Other Termination Chores

Other chores that need to be addressed in this termination phase include:

- Chasing after the electrician to make sure you have electrical outlets where they are required.
- Making sure the satellite dish is installed.
- Installing an FM antenna or an off–air antenna in the attic.
- Identifying any issues with the incoming services, recording those issues on a punch list.

When the termination crew leader walks away from the home at the end of the termination phase, he/she should be able to write a report detailing the remaining items that need to be completed. For example, you might write that the electrician needs to install an electrical outlet in the basement; the cable company still needs to bring in their cables; the telephone company still needs to bring in telephone cables. Then he/she takes the punch list and hands it to your project manager. The project manager can then spend time chasing down the appropriate people to make sure that the work actually happens. Once the internal work is complte the project manager sends out a notice of completion to the customer with an outstanding list of issues with the other trades. A copy is sent to the builder.

Move–In Phase

The last phase in installing a structured wiring system is the move-in phase. The move–in phase should happen within a day or two of your customer moving into the home, and after the service provider has activated the telephone and television. This is the time when you make the home come alive and livable.

Your crew will be working in very clean conditions, so we recommend each member of the team bring in surgical booties for their feet, in addition carry a set of sneakers without laces that are white and new and put on booties over the sneakers. Many builders want you to walk in your socks. If you do that on a regular basis, you could develop painful problems with your feet. So having a very comfortable pair of sneakers with booties that you can easily slip on and off will save you a lot of headache – or foot ache as the case may be.

Once the wallplates are attached, your crew will put blank wallplates over the holes left for the keypads. In order for the builder to get a C.O. (Certificate of Occupancy), there can be no holes in any of the walls. Your team, during the termination phase, has terminated, tested and labeled the keypad cables. The keypads will be installed with the rest of the electronics during the electronics phase. Putting on blank wallplates allows your customer to move in and enjoy their new home.

Another project that is completed in the move–in phase is installation of the architectural speakers in the ceiling or wall. That will take a little bit of time, but the rest of the work is fairly straight forward.

The last thing to do in the move-in phase is making sure all the wallplate connections to the telephones and televisions are working properly. If the distribution panels are prepared properly with quick disconnects, it will be a straight-forward process to go to the incoming cable service and test it. Then test each of the wallplates in the home. We recommend carrying in a small television to test cable television signals. A telephone butt set is also recommended to test the incoming telephone lines.

The television and the telephone are now "live". If the owners have Internet, the move-in team will need to mount their cable modem. We recommend providing a router, hub and patch cables as part of the structured wiring system. The reason we recommend selling these items as part of your system, is that you will be familiar with the products and how they are installed.

Provide the router and switch as rack-mounted devices, and install them as part of your distribution panel. Then all you need is a customer-supplied cable modem. It is to your advantage to install the router and hub in the termination phase.

When you install a cable modem, bring your laptop to test the Internet connection. We strongly recommend against using customer computers to test the Internet connection. You don't know anything about their computers. If you use a customer's computer, you can open a door to all kinds of problems.

Making sure the Internet is "live" is part of your contract. But what if your customer wants you to work with his/her computer? You need to let him/her know that work is outside the limits of your contract. However you should, on a hourly basis, provide an IT (information technology) person. That way the IT person can set up your customer's computers, and plug in their printers and other devices.

That's it for the move-in phase. You've made the home ready to move in. The owners won't have a music system; they won't have a lighting system; they won't have integration. But they won't need those luxuries to move into their new home.

The Other Pieces of Integration

The telephone system and all the other systems that we're going to discuss are all electronics phase items and they will layer on top of our structured wiring system. We've put in an appropriate structured wiring system that will allow you to pop in any of the other systems planned in the home.

The "Satellite Sub-contractor" Letter

NOTES

The letter to the right is a good example of how you can utilize outside contractors to perform specific tasks within your company.

With this letter we are able to accurately determine installation cost and then charge the customer a fair markup. You are passing any of the unknowns on to the subcontractor.

In order to utilize subcontractors effectively you must have a clear line of deliniation between the internal work and subcontractor's work. In this case we are providing a ground block in the attic as a connection point for the satellite installer.

Dear Sirs;

(Company Name) requests that you provide and install an 18"x20" DIRECTV Multi–Satellite dish antenna (Triple–LNB) for (Customer Name).

Please follow the instructions listed below.

1)   Install the dish at the home in the area least visible from the front of the home.

2)   Install four (4) RG6–QD cables from the dish to a ground block mounted in the attic. **We will provide and install the ground block.**

3)   Install a #10 ground wire from the dish to the ground block located in the attic.

4)   Test the installed dish for the minimum acceptable signal strength of 87, as measured at the ground block in the attic. If you cannot attain a signal of this level or higher, please contact me directly to arrange for an acceptable alternative. Measurements should pass on the following satellites; Satellite A, 101 – with transponders #1 to #32. Satellite B, 119 – with transponders #22 to #32, and Satellite C, 110 – with converted transponders #8, #10, #12.

5)   Contact me directly to arrange the installation of a mounting board, if the dish is to be mounted to the siding on the home.

6)   Complete all work by (Date Required). We have a standing agreement of (Dollar Amount).

Please forward your invoice within seven days of completing the project, to my attention, including the customer name, site address, and date of installation. Please fax to (Your Fax Number)

Tools, test equipment, cables, dish, and other supplies are your responsibility and are included in the prearranged price of the installation.

All installations must meet city, county, state and federal standards for installation of low–voltage devices, aerial antennae and satellite dishes.

You are responsible for total cost of damages to equipment, materials, and building systems that were caused during the performance of the work.

All cables that enter the home must include fire–stopping and must conform to both flame and temperature ratings as required by the local building codes and with United Laboratories fire test in a configuration that is representative of field conditions. All penetrations are to be sealed for a minimum F rating of one (1) hour but not less than the fire resistance rating of the assembly being penetrated.

Any work needing to be done that falls outside the original scope of work should be communicated prior to beginning any work at the site. Any out of scope work done without prior approval will not be reimbursed. This approval must come directly from me. Call me immediately and give the details of all time and materials required to complete the installation. You will be notified quickly whether the change order will be approved. An example of a change order would be a chimney or ground mount.

Thank You,

(PM Name)

(Title and Contact Information)

NOTES

NOTES

5

KEYPADS
&
TOUCHSCREENS

What's Inside

One Touch Does It

Creating Scenes & Modes

Specifiying the Programming

Chapter Five

Introduction

A computer terminal is not some clunky old television with a typewriter in front of it. It is an interface where the mind and body can connect with the universe and move bits of it about.

– Douglas Noel Adams (1952–) English humorist and science fiction novelist

What is a Keypad?

A keypad is a device used to provide immediate access to the most relevant functions of the integrated system, such as "On" to turn on the room lights. A keypad, approximately the size of a two- or four–gang box, is designed to be simple. It is limited in its capability. In our proposal we offer two different keypads, a two–button and a six button, each with a different application.

Because of its limitations, many designers try to achieve desired functionality by designing keypads with far too many buttons. The result is a confusing, hard–to–understand user interface. Remember KISS! (Keep it simple stupid.)

What is a Touchscreen?

A touchscreen is a device that has the capability to have many, perhaps hundreds of buttons available to your customer, all designed in a way that is easy to understand. A good touchscreen is designed in multiple layers, so that most relevant commands are on the top layer or level. As the customer moves down through menus the touchscreen will uncover less–used functions. Here is an example.

The TPS–2000 touchscreen has 10 buttons on it, so let's say we take a button and label it "Radio". Touch the "Radio" button, a fre-quently–used command, and it will turn the music on in a room and select the radio. The volume will turn on to a pre–set level, and the last–used radio station will play. The next level menu will appear on the screen allowing the customer to change radio stations. On that page there is a button that allows your customer to go to the next level page to select from pre–set stations. At anytime your customer can return to the main page by touching the main menu button and make other adjustments to the system.

Select a Keypad or a Touchscreen?

Touchscreens are placed in areas of the home where customers spend most of his/her time, such as the kitchen, the master bed-room, and the family room.

Keypads are located in secondary areas, such the dining room or living room. If your customer chooses to integrate his/her music system, and does not integrate the lighting, security, and HVAC sys-tems, then the six–button keypad will provide most of the functional-ity desired throughout most of the home. However, your customer will need a touchscreen in a convenient location to change radio sta-tions, program setup options, and control the music server.

If your customer chooses to integrate lighting, security, and HVAC, the larger touchpanels, such as the TPS–4500, for the main areas of the home, and the smaller touchscreens, such as the TPS–2000, are

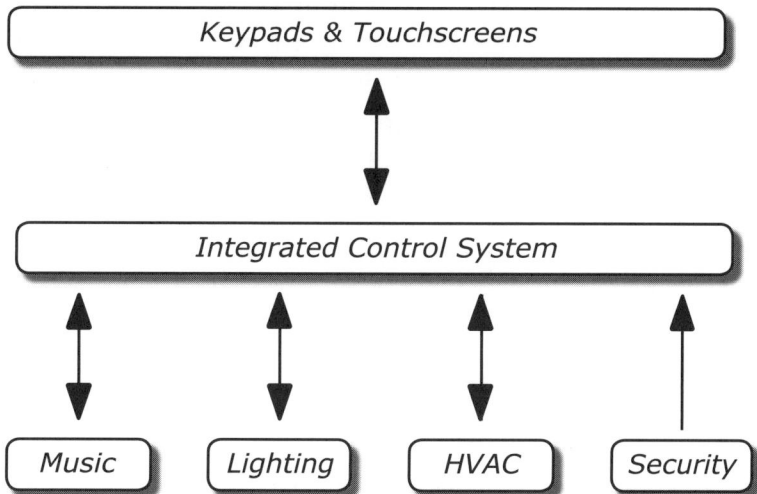

Figure 5.1
Integrated
Control System

Keypads & Touchscreens

Integrated Control System

Music   Lighting   HVAC   Security

125

used in the secondary areas.

What is the Integrated Control System?

An integrated control system acts as an umbrella over all the other systems in the home. This includes the music, lighting, HVAC and security systems. Figure 5.1 shows how these systems to work together. Here are some examples of this interaction:

Security – Your customer leaves his/her home and arms the security system. The RS232 output on the security system will create an event that is interpreted by the integrated control system. The integrated system tells the lighting system, via its RS232 connection, to run the lighting scene designated for "Away". The integrated control system also will turn off the music system, set the thermostats to "Away", and turn off any of the integrated theater systems in the home.

Lighting – Pressing the "Lights" button on the touchscreen will send a command from the touchscreen to the integrated control system, which in turn will send a RS232 command to the lighting control system. It will send a button press command for a virtual keypad, discussed further in this chapter. That button press triggers the lighting scene requested. When the lights reach their programmed level the lighting control system will tell the integrated control system by lighting the LED on the virtual button. The integrated control system then communicates with the touchscreen and the touchscreen highlights a button that looks like an LED to let the customer know the lights are on and at the designated level.

Customer Proposal

NOTES

The keypads & touchscreens should be the foundation of your proposal presentation to your customer. These devices are your customer's primary access point to the services and options of the integrated system. They are the part of the system that your customer will interact with every day in order to enjoy the luxury, convenience and time–saving aspects of the integrated system.

Spend considerable time emphasizing the graphics and easy–to–use nature of the touchscreens. Make a point of bringing a touchscreen with you to your customer presentation. Let your customer examine the sleek lines of the touchscreen, and its smooth surface. In preparing for your presentation, hire a programmer to develop software to enable you to demonstrate the touchscreen's multiple layers of command buttons. A portable power supply connected to the touchscreen can make

Touchscreens and keypads are designed to provide elegance, simplicity and convenience to your busy lifestyle. They are used to control your lights, HVAC, security, music, home theatre and other media devices. Touchscreens are capable of controlling a wide variety of items and are placed in rooms where you want to control everything. Keypads have a few buttons and are used in the remaining rooms to control a few things.

Touchscreens and keypads are used to control your music system and your multimedia devices (HDTV, cable, satellite, DVD, VCR and AM/FM/XM radio and other consumer electronics) throughout your home. They also are used to control your home temperature, lighting and security – all three with the touch of one button.

Your integrated system uses a revolutionary concept to achieve this interoperable capability. This concept uses "scenes" and "modes" to control certain aspects of your system. It may be a new concept for you, and at first the idea of using scenes and modes may seem strange to you and your family, but it will allow you to control the HVAC, lighting and security in your home very simply and easily. And it also integrates certain aspects of your music and theatre systems.

We have designed special modes that are programmed into your touchscreens and keypads to control the multiple systems of your integrated system. We will tailor these modes to match your

NOTES

it possible for your customer to actually see how the touchscreen layers change to reveal different levels of choices.

Also focus on the flexibility of the touchscreen, and how it can be programmed to the way your particular customer wants it programmed. Explain how you will help your customer determine his/her preferences that will be programmed into the touchscreens.

You also can bring an example of a keypad to show your customer how simple they will be to use for music and lighting choices. And how unobtrusive they will be when they are installed at the entrance of a doorway.

preferences, and we will help you through the process of selecting your preferences. Modes can be as varied as your imagination.

Our standard modes include:

Home Mode - Touch the "Home" mode button and it adjusts your lighting the way you want it when you are at home. It also adjusts your heating and cooling system the way you prefer when you're at home. Most homeowners do not include the music system in this mode. They prefer to use a separate keypad for that function. If you have chosen to integrate your security system, when you disarm your alarm system it automatically will trigger the "Home" mode. You need to touch only one button to take care of numerous functions in your entire home.

Night Mode - Touch the "Night" mode button and it adjusts your lighting to the way you want it at night. It also turns off your music system, and adjusts your heating and cooling system to the temperature you want in your home at night. Frequently the "Night" mode is modified to leave certain lights unchanged from the "Home" mode. If you have chosen to integrate your security system, selecting Home Arm on the alarm panel typically triggers the "Night" mode.

Away Mode - Touch the "Away" mode button when you leave your home for the day or for a few hours. It will set the lights to the level you want when you leave your home briefly. It turns off the music system, and adjusts your heating and cooling system to the way you want it for brief absences. If you have chosen to integrate your security system, when you select "Arm

Alarm" it triggers the "Away" mode.

Entertain Mode – Touch the "Entertain" mode button and it sets the lights in your home to the level you want for entertaining. It turns on your music system (Some homeowners want soft music in certain rooms, and other higher volume music in other rooms, perhaps a game room or a ballroom.), and it also adjusts your heating and cooling system to respond to having more people in your home.

Vacation Mode – Touch the "Vacation" mode button when you are leaving your home for more than a few days. It will adjust the lights throughout your home to the way you want them when you are on vacation. It also turns off the music system, and adjusts the heating and cooling system to appropriate levels that you previously have selected. It is also possible for your integrated system to remember your lighting pattern for the previous few weeks, and repeat that pattern automatically when you are on vacation. That way lights in your home turn on and off at various times of the day, making it appear as though someone was at home. This differs from other methods that set lights to turn on and off at the same time every day.

The table below shows a typical system for music, lighting, and HVAC integration. We will work with you during the system programming to further define your needs.

Mode	Music	Lights – Day	Lights – Night	HVAC
Home	No Change	No Change	Floor On Scene	Home
Away	House Off	House Off	House Off	Away
Night	House Off	Night Scene	Night Scene	Night
Entertain	Satellite Soft Rock On	No Change	First Floor On & Outside On	No Change
Vacation	House Off	House Off	House Off	Vacation

Touchscreens

Our Touchscreens can provide access to:

Music Control

- Radio & Satellite Music selections with up to sixteen (16) selections per touchscreen level with an indication of what station is playing already.
- Compact Disc (CD) commands that provide control of transport, groups, and direct selection of the CD position.
- Room selection that controls up to sixteen (16) rooms.
- Status of music displays in up to sixteen (16) rooms.
- Operational control of a music server capable of searching by artist, alblum, and song.

Lighting

- Provides operation of local lighting scenes.
- Indicates status of lighting scenes for up to sixteen (16) rooms.
- Provides access to scenes for all floors, the entire home, and the landscaping areas.

Comfortable Temperatures

- Provides selection of thermostat setbacks for each zone.
- Provides feedback of current temperature in each zone and outside.

Entertain Wizard

- This wizard–style interface will provide the capability to select rooms and a music selection. In addition, you may set the volume of each room and lock out touchscreens to prevent guests from making unwanted changes to the home–wide systems.

System Setup Pages

- Allows you to set key features of the system, such as radio stations, thermostat setpoints, and security lighting options.

Types of Touchscreens and Keypads

We have listed below several types of touchscreens and two types of keypads. We include power supplies, connection terminals, and a distribution panel with your touchscreens and keypads.

TPS–2000L wall–mounted touchscreen – has a five–inch display with a 320 x 240 screen resolution and 10 soft keys.

TPS–3000 touchscreen with video – has a six–inch touchscreen with 640 x 480 screen resolution and five soft keys. This touchscreen has video capability, which can be used to view satellite, cameras, the music server, and cable television. This touchscreen is available as either a wall–mounted or table top version.

TPS–4500 table top – has a state–of–the–art touchscreen with a 12–inch display with a sharp, high resolution picture for both graphics and video.

TPS–4500 wireless upgrade – has two–way wireless communication.

TPS–4500 video upgrade – has video capability for a single video input.

Keypads

Keypads provide fewer options than touchscreens, and generally work in conjunction with touchscreens. They are used in secondary locations to provide access to the integrated system. Keypads are available in white, ivory, and black.

Two–Button Music Keypad – provides volume up and down, and is linked to a touchscreen, which is used to select the music choice.

Two–Button Home–Wide Keypad – provides selection of two

home–wide scenes, such as "Home" and "Away".

Six–Button Music Keypad – controls music in a single room, and typically is located in a room near another room with a touchscreen. While the touchscreen provides complete control of the music system, this keypad provides a small subset for secondary locations. The keypad buttons turn on the music, control volume and the source of the music.

The Controllers

The CP2E Compact Control System – Designed for smaller systems, the CP2E will control three systems of the following type: home theater system, music server, and lighting control. While you may have multiples of each type of system, the CP2E will only support a total of 3 systems. In addition it will control the integrated music system, and an unlimited number of keypads and touchscreens.

The Pro 2 Control System – acts as the heart of the integrated system. It includes the Pro2 control components. This system will control up to six systems of the following type; home theater system, music server, and a lighting control system. While you may have multiples of each type of system, the CP2E will only support a total of 6 systems. In addition it will control the integrated music system, an unlimited number of keypads and touchscreens, and adds the capability of storing user preferences during a power loss.

The Custom Computer – provides remote control of the integrated system. It also allows programming, archiving of documentation and it can be used as a test tool. Also included are an equipment rack, and surge protection, and an uninterruptible power supply (UPS) for short–term power loss or power drops.

Customer Information

The table below is used to show the location of each keypad and touchscreen in your home. We will assist you in completing this table. Then we will place "cabling" stickers in your home in the specific location indicated for each keypad and touchscreen. This will give you an opportunity to approve all locations before the cables are actually installed in your home.

Location	Keypad and/or Touchscreen
Kitchen	TPS-3000 In-Wall Touchscreen
Breakfast Rm	
Study	TPS-3000 In-Wall Touchscreen
Living Rm	TPS-2000 In-Wall Touchscreen
Dining Rm	TPS-2000 In-Wall Touchscreen
Family Rm	
Deck	Two-Button Keypad
Garage	
Master Bdrm	TPS-3000 In-Wall Touchscreen
Master Bath	TPS-2000 In-Wall Touchscreen
Bedroom 2	TPS-2000 In-Wall Touchscreen
Bedroom 3	TPS-2000 In-Wall Touchscreen
Bedroom 4	TPS-2000 In-Wall Touchscreen
Theater Rm	
Game Rm	

Figure 5.2
Keypad & Touch-
sreen Locations

Your Control System	Pro2 with the custom computer
Integrated Systems	Lighting, Music, HVAC, and Security

Figure 5.3
System
Options

133

Specifying the Programming

The following information involves the programming for the entire system. We put it all in this section rather than in each individual chapter about a partticular system.

The information below can be handed directly to the programming company to program the system for your customer. Very shortly after the printing of this book www.dipartner.com will be selling code blocks for this specification. While we are basing this chapter around the Crestron system, you can use this specification with very little change for other systems, such as those from AMX and other brands of integration.

You do not need to be able to program any of these systems in order to install and service them. We have included in this chapter a specification for a computer to place in the equipment rack with the customer system. This will allow your programmer to interface with the system and make changes remotely.

This book's download will contain a complete set of specifications to provide to your programming company.

Home Layout

The first step in specifying the programming is to lay out locations for lighting keypads, music zones, and thermostat addresses in the home. The table below specifies the locations and how they relate to the thermostats, lighting keypads, and music zones.

Floor	Room	Lighting Keypad	Music Zone	Thermostat Address
1	Kitchen	1	1	1
1	Breakfast room	2	2	1
1	Study	3	3	2
1	Living room	4	4	1
1	Dining room	5	5	1

1	Family room	6	6	1
1	Deck	7	7	
1	Garage	8		
2	Master bdrm.	9	8	3
2	Master bath	10	9	3
2	Bedroom 2	11	10	4
2	Bedroom 3	12	11	4
2	Bedroom 4	13	12	4
B	Theater room	14	13	5
B	Game room	15	14	6
L	Landscape 1	29		
L	Landscape 2	30		
	Home–wide 1	31		
	Home–wide 2	32		

Figure 5.4
Home Layout Table

Mode Specifications

Modes affect the entire home and multiple systems with a single touch. By touching the "Home" button you can change the lighting, temperature, and music in the home. This is where the integration of these systems comes together. In order to keep the system easy–to–operate we recommend that it is the only place where your customer can touch one button to combine the multiple systems. We define a scene that affects changes to a single system. A mode affects changes to multiple systems. Below is an explanation or specification of each mode.

Day–Home – This mode is designed for daylight hours when someone is at home. If the "Home" button is pressed on any keypad or touchscreen, it will select the "Day–Home" prior to sunset and the "Night–Home" after sunset, and the "Overnight–Home" after the time specified for bedtime.

Night–Home – This mode is designed for after sunset, however before bedtime in the home.

Overnight–Home – This mode is designed for bedtime hours in the home. This may be activated by the security system, by selecting "Arm to Home" on the security system. See the security system programming for more on this.

Away – This mode is used when the residents of the home are away from the home for a short period of time, for example to go to work or school for the day.

Vacation – This mode is used when the residents of the home leave the home for an extended period of time, generally a few days or more.

Entertain – This mode is used when the residents of the home are entertaining a group of people in the home. The setup page will allow the customer to disable all touchscreens and keypads in the home except for the kitchen panel. This will prevent accidental changes in the lighting, music, and HVAC systems.

Figure 5.5 shows mode settings for music, lighting, and HVAC integration. See each system chapter for more details.

Mode	Music	Lighting Scene	HVAC
Day–Home	No Change	No Change	Home
Night–Home	No Change	Night–Home	Home
Overnight–Home	System Off	Overnight–Home	Overnight
Away	System Off	Away	Away
Vacation	System Off	Vacation	Vacation
Entertain	Entertain	Entertain	Home

Figure 5.5 Home Modes

Lighting Touchscreen Programming

The lighting touchscreen programming is responsible for a number of functions. It

• Provides the operation of local and remote lighting.

• Indicates the status of lighting scenes in up to sixteen (16) rooms.

- Provides access to scenes for all floors

The Virtual Lighting Keypad

The virtual keypads are non–existent as actual keypads in the home; they only exist in the programming of the lighting control system. As such, on the computer you can touch these virtual buttons to trigger lighting scenes.

Figure 5.6 shows the programming for virtual lighting keypads, each of which has 15 virtual buttons.

Button	Scene	Button	Scene	Button	Scene
1	Room – Full On	6		11	
2	Room – Day	7		12	
3	Room – Night	8		13	
4	Room – Soft	9		14	
5	Room – Off	10		15	

Figure 5.6
Lighting
Keypad

Full On – This turns on every light in the room to 87%.   This scene has been designed for cleaning the room. Note: The human eye cannot perceive any difference between 87% and 100% lighting, Setting to 87% will appear to be fully on, yet conserve electricity.

Room–Day – This turns on the lighting in the room to the day scene. The day lighting needs are slightly higher than at night time so this scene is typically set to higher levels than the night scene. A touchscreen can learn lighting scenes. This is accomplished by activating the scene from the touchscreen, then adjusting the individual dimmers in the room to the desired level, then touching the "Store Scene" button on the touchscreen. Another page on the touchscreen will ask if these settings are to be saved to the "Room–Day", "Room–Night", or "Room–Soft" scene.

137

Room–Night – This scene is similar to the "Room–Day" scene; however, it is designed to be activated after sunset.

Room–Soft – This scene has two purposes. 1. It is activated in am unoccupied room to give it minimal lighting for someone to walk through it safely without being in the dark, and to give the home added dimension and warmth. 2. It is activated during the overnight–home mode to dimly light a bedroom for getting out of bed in the middle of the night. It too can be stored from a touch-screen.

Buttons 6 to 15 allow expansion beyond the standard programming template. In addition to the standard virtual keypad, there are several special keypads, each of which has 15 virtual buttons.

Btn	Scene	Btn	Scene	Btn	Scene
1	All – Full On	6	Front – Full On	11	Back – Full On
2	All – Sunrise	7	Front – Sunrise	12	Back – Sunrise
3	All – Sunset	8	Front – Sunset	13	Back – Sunset
4	All – Overnight	9	Front – Overnight	14	Back – Overnight
5	All – Off	10	Front – Off	15	Back – Off

Figure 5.7 Landscape 1 Keypad

Btn	Scene	Btn	Scene	Btn	Scene
1	Garage – Full On	6	Non Garage Side – Full On	11	
2	Garage – Sunrise	7	Non Garage Side – Sunrise	12	
3	Garage – Sunset	8	Non Garage Side – Sunset	13	
4	Garage – Overnight	9	Non Garage Side – Overnight	14	
5	Garage – Off	10	Non Garage Side – Off	15	

Figure 5.8 Landscape 2 Keypad

Figure 5.9 Home 1 Keypad

Btn	Scene	Btn	Scene	Btn	Scene
1	1st Floor – On	6	2nd Floor – On	11	House – On
2	1st Floor – Day	7	2nd Floor – Day	12	House – Day

Btn	Scene	Btn	Scene	Btn	Scene
3	1st Floor – Night	8	2nd Floor – Night	13	House – Night
4	1st Floor – Soft	9	2nd Floor – Soft	14	House – Soft
5	1st Floor – Off	10	2nd Floor – Off	15	House – Off

Btn	Scene	Btn	Scene	Btn	Scene
1	Basement – On	6	Entertain	11	Vacation – Record
2	Basement – Day	7		12	Vacation – Play
3	Basement – Night	8		13	Vacation – Stop
4	Basement – Soft	9		14	
5	Basement – Off	10		15	

Figure 5.10
Home 2
Keypad

The Two–Button Keypad

Modes Application – This keypad is used to activate one of two modes. For example, you can place a two–button keypad in the garage by the entrance to the home and use it to activate the "Home" and "Away" modes. Another example is placing a keypad by the bed in the master bedroom with the "Day–Home" mode labeled as "Morning" and the "Overnight–Home" labeled as "Bed-time".

Location	Button 1	Button 2
Garage	"Home" Mode	"Away" Mode
Master Bedroom	"Day–Home" Mode	"Overnight–Home" Mode

Figure 5.11
Two–Button
Keypad

Volume Application – The top button will provide volume up and if the zone is off it will turn on and sync its source to another zone. The bottom button will provide volume down and when the volume goes below a critical level (pre–set on the setup page of the touchscreen); it will shut off the zone. A great place to locate this keypad is in the dining room, with it synchronizing its source to the kitchen. And if the kitchen is turned off, the zone will de-fault to a specified source in the setup page of the touchscreen.

139

Figure 5.12
Two–Button
Keypad

Location	Button 1	Button 2
Dining Room	Zone 3 Vol. Up	Zone 3 Vol. Down
Living Room	Zone 4 Vol. Up	Zone 3 Vol. Down
3–Season Porch	Zone 5 Vol. Up	Zone 3 Vol. Down

The Six Button Keypad

Music Application –This keypad is designed to control music in a single room. Typically it is located in a room near another room with a touchscreen. While the touchscreen provides complete control of the music system, this keypad will provide a small subset for secondary locations. The keypad buttons are as follows:

Figure 5.12
Six–Button
Keypad

Button	Function	Button	Function
1	Select Radio	4	Vol. Up
2	Select Sat Receiver	5	Vol. Down
3	Select Music Server	6	Room On/Off

Touchscreen Music Programming

FM Radio –The FM radio is programmed to work the same as a car radio with eight pre–set stations that the customer can store. This is accomplished only if you use the integrated FM tuner from Crestron as part of the integrated system.

XM Radio – Programmed to select from one of sixteen user– selected stations from any of the system touchscreens. These stations are set as part of the system programming. Both a Crestron C2N–TXM XM radio receiver and a monthly subscription for the music are needed.

Direct TV for Music – Programmed to select from one of sixteen user–selected stations from any of the system touchscreens. These stations are set as part of the system programming. This option requires a Direct TV satellite receiver that is dedicated to music, and a monthly subscription for the music.

Preset	Station	Preset	Station
1	804 - Radio Disney	9	816 - Metal
2	806 - Seasonal	10	817 - Alternative
3	808 - Reggae	11	818 - Rock
4	809 - Classic R&B	12	819 - Classic Rock
5	813 - Dance	13	823 - '80s
6	814 - Retro	14	824 - '70s
7	815 - Arena Rock	15	822 - Hit List

Figure 5.13
Direct TV
Station List

Digital Cable for Music – Programmed to select from one of sixteen user defined stations from any of the system touchscreens. These stations are set as part of the system programming. This option requires a Direct TV satellite receiver that is dedicated to music, and a monthly subscription for the music. Unfortunately cable companies change the stations frequently, will require reprogramming.

Preset	Station	Preset	Station
1	504 - Radio Disney	9	516 - Metal
2	506 - Seasonal	10	517 - Alternative
3	508 - Reggae	11	518 - Rock
4	509 - Classic R&B	12	519 - Classic Rock
5	513 - Dance	13	523 - '80s
6	514 - Retro	14	524 - '70s
7	515 - Arena Rock	15	522 - Hit List

Figure 5.13
Digital Cable
Station List

CD Player – Touchscreens will include control over the current disc as well as the capability to select any of the six discs.

Digital Music Server – Unfortunately not every function within the music server lends itself to a touchscreen. When creating and editing play lists, including file tags and genre designation, the task is performed from a personal computer. The music server is connected to the home network, so all that has to be done is to upload the server program on the customer's computer. Below is a list of functionality groups, and how they can be accessed.

Zone & Room	FM Radio 1	FM Radio 2	FM Radio 3	CD	Music Serv-er 1	Music Zone	Music Serv-er 2	XM Radio 1	XM Radio 2	XM Radio 3
1 – Kitchen	X				X			X		
2 – Breakfast rm.	X				X			X		
3 – Study	X				X			X		
4 – Living rm.	X				X			X		
5 – Dining rm.	X				X			X		
6 – Family rm.										
7 – Deck	X				X			X		
8 – Master bdrm.		X				X			X	
9 – Master bath		X				X			X	
10 – Bedroom 2			X				X			X
11 – Bedroom 3			X				X			X
12 – Bedroom 4			X				X			X
13 – Theater rm.										
14 – Game room			X				X			X

Figure 5.15
Music Source
Selection

Play lists – Select any of the user–selected play lists.

Search – Search by artist, album, or song.

Basic Play List Edit – Remove all songs from a play list and add individual songs.

Advanced Play List Edit – Edit all song information to include artist, album name, genre, and MP3 file tags. In addition create play lists.

Feature	Touch-screens	Touchscreens with video	Personal Computer
Basic play lists	X	X	X
Search	X	X	X
Basic play list Edit		X	X
Advanced Edit			X

Figure 5.14
Digital Server
Functionality

Music Source Selections

Figure 5.15 specifies what sources will play in what sections of the home. In this scenario the owners are requesting a set of sources for the first floor and common areas, a second set for the master suite, and a third for the children's areas of the home. The music zone will be connected to the first server that serves the common areas, however it will be zoned with the master suite.

Entertain wizard – This wizard style interface will provide the capability to select rooms and a music selection. In addition you may set the volume of each room and lock out touchscreens to prevent guests from making unwanted changes to the home–wide systems.

HVAC Touchscreen Programming

• Provides selection of HVAC mode for each zone with feedback of current temperature in each zone and outside.

• Provides a selection with Room Off that provides a "Music Off" and "Lights Off" in that room.

• Provides status and selection of all modes.

143

Building the Computer

Why should you include a computer as part of your integrated system?

The computer is a test and diagnostic tool. It allows the technician to test audio and video signals in the equipment rack. It includes a TV card. You can plug a cable from the CATV panel to test the cable signal without leaving the electronics closet. The video input on the TV card should be connected to a satellite receiver to test and activate satellite for the customer.

In order to use this tool, you must have a completed home network in the home. It should contain a cable modem for high-speed internet access, a router (8-port) to share the cable modem, and a switch to connect multiple computers to the router in the home, if more than eight machines are present in the home. In addition we recommend installing a 4-port hub inside the equipment rack to connect the music servers and the computer, so that a single networking connection is all that is needed.

You can purchase the following from Thompson's Computer Warehouse, www.TCWO.com. The company representatives will even assemble the hardware for you. While the following list of equipment will be outdated by the time you read this book, it can be used as a guideline to purchasing the correct pieces for your computer. We have included a specification to send to your computer provider for bid purposes. We recommend setting an $800 cost budget for the computer.

- Rack mount chassis (Black) – Antec rack mount case 4U

- Keyboard (Black) – PS/2

- Mouse (Black) – PS/2

- Speakers (Black) –

- Monitor (Black) – 17 inch 0.23HDP

- CD Rom (Black) – Samsung 52x

- Motherboard – ATX with integrated A/V and networking, MSI KM4M–L

- Processor – AMD Duron 1.6 GHz

- Processor Fan Kit – Coolmaster DPS–6IB1D

- Hard Drive – Maxtor 40GB

- RAM – 256 Meg DDR, PC2100, 266 MHz

- TV Card – MSI TV anywhere Master TV/FM tuner

- Microsoft Windows XP Pro – OEM version

The following is a list of software to install on the computer.

From **www.microsoft.com**

Microsoft Word Viewer (Free) – Used to view Word files.

Microsoft Power Point Viewer (Free) – Used to view Power Point files.

Microsoft Excel Viewer (Free) – Used to view Excel files.

From **www.adobe.com**

Adobe Acrobat (Free) – Used to view PDF files.

From **www.winzip.com**

Winzip trial version (Free) – Used to compact and uncompact files for emailing and uploading to your companies FTP site

From **www.tzo.com**

My Wan IP ($50/year) – Used to determine WAN IP address of the home. This will allow you to create a website name for a customer on the web and have it point to the customer's home. Every time the cable modem in the home changes IP address the software will automatically update the link information.

From **www.wsftp.com**

WS FTP (Free) – Used to setup an FTP server on the computer. This is a password protected file area of the computer used to transfer files to and from the computer.

From **www.winvnc.com**

Win VNC (Free) – Used to take control of the desktop from an internet browser anywhere in the world. This allows your software engineer to diagnose problems, make changes, and update software without the need of traveling to the customer's home. This will require opening two ports on your router, port 5800 and port 5900; in addition you will need to forward those ports to the internal static IP address of the computer.

In addition you will need to load all of the owner manuals, installation manuals, and programming manuals for each of your vendors. We suggest that you collect this information on your server to facilitate setting up the computer. You will also need to install the proprietary software for each of your vendors. Install and copy everything, even if the customer is not getting that particular device. This will facilitate upgrades a later date.

N O T E S

NOTES

N O T E S

6

MUSIC
INTEGRATION

What's Inside

Zones & Groups

Focusing on Sound

Music, Music, Musc

Chapter Six

Introduction

> *The only things in my life that compatibly exist with this grand universe are the creative works of the human spirit.*
>
> *– Ansel Adams (1902––1984) US landscape photographer, conservationist.*

The home–wide music system distributes tunes from one centralized music system to speakers installed discretely throughout the home. There are basically two types of home–wide music systems from which to choose: a system that distributes the same song to every speaker, or a more intelligent system that allows each family member to listen to a different music source (such as a CD player and tuner) simultaneously in different rooms.   We will focus on the latter of the two systems. Since this book is designed as an integration resource, our focus will be on integrating the music system into the overall system. We also have included a brief synopsis on designing your music system.

Where to Locate Speakers

The must–have speaker locations are the kitchen, living room, dining room, study, deck/patio on the back of the home, and master bedroom and bath.

The secondary speaker locations include the other bedrooms, the garage, the children's recreation area and the laundry room.

The family room speakers are typically part of a separate surround sound system, which calls for a surround sound wallplate to be installed as part of the structured wiring system. If your customer does not want a surround sound system installed, you can use the rear channel speaker cabling to add this room to the centralized music system.

Zones and Groups

There are two reasons for creating zones in your music system.

Different source – Each zone is capable of using its own source. It is possible to play music from the music server in one room and the FM radio in another. We suggest that you divide the home into groups of rooms that share the same source.

Different volume level – Even though two rooms share a common source for music, your customer may want selections playing at two volume levels. For this reason we suggest that you create a separate zone for each room in the home. That means each room can have its own volume levels. If you attempt to share two rooms in a single zone, both rooms will have the same volume. Once you have established separate zones for each room, you can use the software to create room groups that share the same source. Yes, you could add volume controls to these rooms, but these two rooms would have a different interface than the rest of the home, which can result in a confusing system.

Floor	Room	Group	Zone
1	Kitchen	1	1
1	Breakfast rm.	1	2
1	Study	2	3
1	Living rm.	1	4
1	Dining rm.	1	5
1	Family rm.	3	6
1	Deck	1	7
2	Master bdrm.	4	8
2	Master bath	4	9
2	Bedroom 2	5	10
2	Bedroom 3	6	11
2	Bedroom 4	7	12
B	Theater room	8	13
B	Game room	8	14

Figure 6.1
Zone & Group
Assignment

Different Types of Speakers

Home speakers are grouped into three categories.

Architectural Speakers – are designed to fit into the décor of the home. They consist of models that fit into the wall, ceiling, and even the outdoors. It is this type of speaker that will be used throughout the home. In-ceiling speakers are the favorite of most customers, and with today's technology, customers can enjoy high quality sound with very little visible presence of equipment in the home.

Traditional Music Speakers – are the speakers that you would normally purchase at your local audio/video retailer. Bookshelf speakers are favorites for locations like the study and other areas of the home with build-in cabinetry. Tower speakers allow the customer to enjoy the highest quality sound level, while retaining some of the advantages of a centralized music system. Place these speakers in formal listening areas, which often is a study or library. In cabling these speakers, it is necessary to change from your standard practice. Instead, run four (4), 14-gauge conductor cables from the electronics closet directly to each speaker. That means you will install four (4) conductors for each speaker. This will allow you to combine the cables into two (2) conductors or to bi-wire the speaker for improved performance. Match these tower speakers with a high quality amplifier for the best sound result.

Home Theater Speakers – consist of a set of speakers that are designed to work together to recreate the theater experience in the home. These speakers are not normally used to listen to music, and are discussed further in the "Theater" chapter.

Should You Add a Subwoofer?

A subwoofer provides enhanced bass to the music output. We recommended that rather than installing subwoofers, it is better to choose a higher quality of speakers for that location. Adding the subwoofer will increase the complexity of the cabling, amplification, and create issues about how to crossover and equalize the subwoofer with the speakers. Reserve the subwoofer for the theater room.

Where to Place the Speakers

Placing and installing speakers for a home–wide music system is both an art and a science. For foreground music applications, place the speakers in the room in such a way as to provide stereo left and right imaging when you are facing the main feature of the room. This feature could be a large picture window or fireplace.

For background music, speakers installed in the ceiling usually provide the best dispersion in any space. These speakers are typically placed in line with ceiling lights. In a bedroom, the best place for the speakers is over the foot of the bed. Always face the speakers toward the main sitting area of the room.

Try to keep speakers at least two feet from any corner in the room. The exceptions are soffit locations because soffits represent extruded room boundaries. They can be used to your advantage to amplify and focus the sound.

In a room with considerably more space than other rooms in the home, it may be necessary to install additional speakers to gain smooth coverage and balanced sound levels. Sometimes smaller spaces actually need more speakers. Speakers installed into a low ceiling may have insufficient distance to properly disperse and attain even sound coverage because of the relatively short distance from the speaker to the listener,.

In any room, bear in mind, that sound propagation is very similar to that of light (angle of incidence equals angle of reflection). A qualified audio system designer can use this information to make a room "sound" larger or more intimate, much the same way as a lighting designer uses lighting to define a room's ambiance and establish comfort.

Where to Locate the Music System

The music system should always be located in the electronics closet in the basement, or other area that is out of sight from the living areas of the home. The components are mounted in an equipment rack, which we explain in detail the chapter, "Keypads and Touchscreens". The amplifiers will generate a good deal of heat, so ensure adequate ventilation. The equipment also needs to be installed in a manner that permits service. If you place the home–wide stereo in a cabinet in the family room, it will overheat, and it will be a bear to install and service. Don't make that mistake! The HVAC contractor would never allow the customer to specify where to put the heating system, so why should you allow the customer to tell you where to put the music system?

Using the remote music and input wallplate described in the "Structured Wiring" chapter allows you to install the CD player anywhere in the home so the homeowner can load his/her discs without having to go to the electronics closet.

The Digital Music Server

The Main Server – is where the CDs are loaded into the system. We are recommending that you use an Audio Request Fusion Pro Music Server. It is typically located inside the equipment rack. However, you can locate it elsewhere in the home by using a remote music and video input wallplate described in the chapter, "Structured Wiring".

Additional Music Zone – is used to provide another location in the home to play CD selections independently from the Music Server. Both the main server and the additional zone are programmed identically.

Adding an Additional Zone or a Server?

A second server (or more) has a separate set of music selections loaded into its system. This is perfect for teenage children, who have their own taste in music. If you provide a server dedicated to their music taste, then when the parents are searching the server they will not hear unwanted music. That makes searching music simpler for both the parents and teens.

On the other hand, if you want to have the same set of music choices throughout the home, but want to have separate zones then add an additional zone.

Customer Proposal

N O T E S

The music sources are separated by zone within the home. This is shown in figure 5.15 in the "Keypads & Touch-screens" chapter. It all lows you to specify what sources play in what rooms or "zones" of the home.

Our integrated digital music system can deliver audio and video to each room, each floor, and each area of your home. Our smart zone system allows you to choose from all your audio and video options – DVD, satellite, CDs, AM/ FM radio, and others – from any touchscreen in your home. You tell us what you want and we design special buttons on your touchscreens that give you immediate access to the programming you want. Your favorite tunes or movies are just a button touch away. Our music system is fully compatible with your integrated control system, and it can:

Distribute up to eight (8) audio sources options – satellite, CD, AM/ FM radio, and others throughout your home.

Play music from multiple sources at the same time.

Play at separate volumes in separate rooms.

Be controlled just by touching a button on a touchscreen.

Turn off when you leave the house just by touching the "Away" button on your touchscreen.

Listening Options

We have listed numerous options below that you can choose to include in your home music system to enhance your listening pleasure.

AM Radio – Your music system will include a radio configured to allow you to select up to thirty (30) AM channels from any of your system touchscreens located where you want them. We will install the AM tuner in your attic to capture the strongest signal available for clear, distinct reception.

FM Radio – The standard fare is two (2) FM tuners for your home. You can select one station to listen to in your home office, while your teenager can select another from his or her bedroom. The keypads and touchscreens, strategically located throughout your home, provide direct access to ten (10) pre–selected favorite stations. Your system also is configured to allow you to select up to thirty (30) other FM channels from any of your system's touchscreens

CD Player – A disc carousel allows you to load up to six (6) discs while one is still playing to give you uninterrupted listening. The changing mechanism is smooth and quiet. The CD player communicates flawlessly with our control systems.

Digital Cable for Music – We will configure your digital cable box to fit seamlessly into your music system. You will be able to select up to thirty (30) cable channels of music from any of your system's touchscreens.

Direct TV for Music – We will install a digital satellite receiver, and we will configure it to provide commercial–free digital music. You will be able to select up to thirty (30) satellite channels of music from any of the system touchscreens.

XM Radio – We will install a specialized XM Radio receiver that can provide commercial–free digital music. You can select up to thirty (30) channels of music from any of your system's touchscreens.

Sirius Triple Play Digital Radio – Triple Play let's you select from sixty (60) different music channels, 24 hours a day, 7 days a week. You can hear all types of music from today's hits to R&B to oldies to classical masterpieces; Triple Play also gives you instant access to more than forty (40) channels of world class news, sports and entertainment. And what's more, Triple Play provides programming for three (3) independent listening zones. That means you can listen to sports, your spouse can listen to an opera, and your son or daughter can listen to rock and roll – all at the same time on the same music system in three different areas of your home.

Music Server – Includes an Audio Request Fusion Pro Music Server specially configured to store your CDs in a central location. From any touchscreen you can select any of the your play lists; search by artist, album, or song; remove all songs from a play list; and add individual songs. In addition from your personal computer you can edit all song information to include artist, album name, genre, and MP3 file tags, and create play lists.

Additional Music Zone – Provides another location in your home to play a CD selection independent of the Music Server. If you prefer, we can load your CDs for you. Three weeks before the installation of your electronic components, provide us with your CDs, and we'll load them all in time for your installation. An additional fee will be charged for this service.

Amplification

Amplifiers produce an even sound from all speakers. Without amplification, the sound would diminish depending on the number of speakers on the system.

Background for Six Speaker Pairs – Includes the a 12–Channel Amplifier delivering 30

NOTES

Group your amplifiers into levels. This allows you to get past the notion of brand name and makes for an easy–to–understand proposal.

The same is done for the speakers.

Watts of power to each channel. This level of amplification is adequate in rooms providing background music.

Hi–fi for Six Speaker Pairs – Includes the a 12–Channel Amplifier, delivering 50 Watts of power to each channel. High fidelity music sounds best when adequate amplification is used.

Hi–fi for One Speaker Pair – Includes the a 2–Channel Amplifier, delivering 60 Watts of power to each channel. High fidelity music sounds best when adequate amplification is used.

High–End for One Speaker Pair – Includes one of a wide variety of amplifiers to meet exacting music requirement. Includes Ultralink Competition audio interconnects for better performance.

Speakers

Architectural speakers are designed to fit into the décor of your home. They consist of models that fit into the wall, ceiling, and even the outdoors. It is this type of speaker that will be used throughout your home. In–ceiling speakers are the favorite of most customers, and with today's technology, customers can enjoy high quality sound with very little visible presence of equipment in your home. We have divided these architectural speakers into three different value points. In addition we have included the High–End speaker category to provide traditional music speakers with various pricing.

Entry Level Speakers – Select these speakers for areas where low–level music is desired.

Background Speakers – Select these speakers for areas where good background music is desired.

Hi–fidelity Speakers – Select these speakers for areas where the quality of the sound is more important.

High–End Speakers – We provide loudspeakers with superior sound quality, design and finish. Includes 14–guage high quality speaker cable, and a finished wallplate.

Customer Information

The table below shows each speaker and its associated amplifier in your home. We will field locate each speaker pair in the rooms shown below with a "cabling" sticker. This will give you an opportunity to approve all locations before the home is cabled.

NOTES

The table to the right shows what type and level of speaker and amplifer will be chosen within the home.

It does not specify a brand for most locations. This is done to focus the customer on the quality level of sound, and not get caught up in the branding of the speakers.

You are selling a solution to your customer, not product! If you carry several brands of architectural speakers, you should be able to attract him/her to one of those brands.

The execption to this is the High End catagory which allows your customer to have his favorite brand speakers in those special locations in the home.

Floor	Room	Speaker Selection	Amplifier Selection
1	Kitchen	Ceiling – Background	Background
1	Breakfast Room	Ceiling – Background	Background
1	Study	Brand XYZ – High End	
1	Living Room	Ceiling – Hi–Fidelity	Hi–Fidelity
1	Dining Room	Ceiling – Hi–Fidelity	Hi–Fidelity
1	*Family Room		
1	Deck	Outdoor –Background	Background
1	Garage		
2	Master bdrm.		Hi–Fidelity
2	Master bath	Ceiling – Background	Background
2	Bedroom 2	Ceiling – Background	Background
2	Bedroom 3	Ceiling – Background	Background
2	Bedroom 4	Wall – Hi–Fidelity	Hi–Fidelity
B	**Theater		
B	Game room	Ceiling – Hi–Fidelity	Hi–Fidelity

*Family Room – The speakers and amplifiers in this room are presented as part of a seperate proposal for the "Family Room Surround Sound System".

**Theater – The speakers and amplifiers in this room are presented as part of a seperate proposal for the "Theater Room System".

Source Selections

The table below lists the music sources which will be available through your system. These sources will be allocated to select rooms in the home, so that your family will not interupt each other with their music choices.

FM Radio 1	Kitchen, Breakfast, Living, Dining, Deck
FM Radio 2	Master Bedroom, Master Bathroom
AM Tuner	Not included
XM Radio	All rooms
Digital Cable for Music	Not included
Direct TV for music	Not included
CD Player (located in family room)	All rooms
Music Server	Kitchen, Breakfast, Living, Dining, Deck, Family Room
Music Server Zone	Master Bedroom, Master Bathroom
Music Source (Mstr Bd TV)	Master Bedroom

Steps to Music Integration

Proposal Process

In presenting a music system to your customer, it is unimportant to determine every model of speaker. Instead we suggest using categories of speakers to determine a working budget for speakers in the home.

Place the emphasis on providing a solution to your customer's listening pleasure. You are providing high quality music throughout the home with simple–to-use keypads and touchscreens.

Let the source selection dictate the need for an integrated control system. Ask them how will they select from their eight favorite radio stations? How will they select that Christmas digital music station on XM radio? If your customer wants to have his/her CD collection in a hard disc system to provide easy access, then they will most certainly need a touchscreen to select artists and songs.

Project Open

The first step is to "Sticker" the home with the "cabling" stickers for each speaker location. While walking the home, determine if ceiling, wall, or bookshelf speakers are needed in the room. You will need to know what millwork cabinets are to be installed in the room. If permanent bookshelves go in the study, then bookshelf speakers will be a better choice than in-ceiling speakers. You also will need to know how far door jams and crown molding will extend out from the wall so that keypads, touchscreens, and speakers will not interfere with the millwork.

Cabling

We discuss cabling in detail in the chapter, "Structured Wiring". Make sure you have allowed enough room in your electronics closet for the music system equipment rack. It should be located at least four feet away from the wall. This will provide adequate room to service the system.

Termination

We discuss termination in detail in the chapter "Structured Wiring". speaker, keypad and touchscreen cables are terminated, tested, and labeled. The distribution panel for the touchscreens also is installed.

Move–In

We discuss the move-in phase in detail in the chapter "Structured Wiring". Speakers are installed; keypad and touchscreen locations are covered with blank wallplates.

Programming & Equipment Build

We discuss the programming and building the equipment in detail in the chapter, "Keypads & Touchscreens". In this phase you will meet with the customer; gather all of the programming information; build the system; and give your customer an opportunity to operate the system prior to installation.

Electronics

If all of the previous phases have been organized and completed, the electronics phase will proceed without difficulty. In this phase the equipment rack is wheeled into the home and connected to a pre-labeled bundle of cables. The keypads & touchscreens, which are labeled by room, are installed. The system is turned on and equipment is ready to use. Any minor issues are worked out at this time, prior to the customer experiencing the system.

Training

Good design will minimize the required training for your customer. Ensure the entire family is available during the training and presentation of the music system.

NOTES

NOTES

NOTES

7

LIGHTING INTEGRATION

What's Inside

What is Lighting

Dimming the light

Designing the lighting control

Steps to installing the lighting control

Chapter Seven

What is Lighting?

And there was light.

Genesis, Chapter 1:3

Since before Adams and Eve, light has been an essential ingredient of our daily lives. In the beginning, there was only sunlight that bathed the world in light and warmth. Torches brought portability of light and the ability bring to light into our homes. Lanterns fueled by coal oil brought additional advantages to both indoor and outdoor lighting. And finally Thomas Alva Edison burst on the scene with electric light.

Today, lighting is both practical and luxurious. It allows you to function in your home and it can bath you in a feeling of warmth and security. Lighting helps you to enjoy all the features of your home to the fullest. It can highlight a favored piece of art, brighten a bookshelf, shine brightly for arriving guests, or dim for a cozy comfortable night of watching TV. It adds grace and beauty to your home. Picture multi–colored prisms of light sparkling from a glass chandelier in your dining room or soft lighting falling on a small intimate group of friends as you entertain in your living room. Light can also provide a dramatic touch to any room. It can help provide a relaxing mood at the end of a hard day at work. Lighting enhances our lives in so many ways, and at a relatively inexpensive cost.

Three Basic Types of Lighting

Three basic types of lighting are used to brighten your home: general, task and accent lighting. A well designed lighting plan combines all three types to meet both function and style.

General Lighting provides overall illumination to any area in your customer's home. It is fundamental to any lighting plan. Basically, it is provided with overhead ceiling lights, chandeliers, wall–mounted lights, and recessed or track lights. Outside your home, lanterns provide general lighting. General lighting, sometimes called ambient lighting, provides enough light to allow you to see and move safely about your home.

Task Lighting allows your customer to read, do homework, write checks, play games, follow recipes for your favorite dish, and build model airplanes or enjoy other hobbies your customer may have. Basically, it is provided by portable lighting (table lights), pendant lighting (hanging lights) or recessed and track lighting. The best task lighting has little or no glare, little or no shadowing, and is bright enough to prevent eyestrain.

Accent Lighting brings drama into the home. It highlights that favorite piece of art, a painting or sculpture, or a favorite Chinese artifact or other prized possession. It can highlight bookshelves, draperies, or the texture of an accent wall. It can also provide visual interest for your customer's outdoor landscaping plan. Accent lighting provides at least three times as much lighting on what it highlights than the general lighting surrounding it. It is usually provided by wall–mounted fixtures, track or recessed lighting.

Selecting a Lighting Fixture

In selecting lighting fixtures for the home, there are many types of choices to enhance any décor. Your customers will need to know what type of fixture is best for the area or object they want to light. For example, general lighting in the foyer is accomplished by using a ceiling light or recessed light. To highlight artwork, they select a wall–mounted fixture. Then your customer's decorator, architect, lighting designer, or local lighting supply house will help select the actual fixture from a plethora of choices. The different types of fixtures are listed below.

Ceiling– or Surface–mounted Fixtures – most commonly used for general lighting, basically replacing sunlight. A practical lighting solution, they are best used in kitchens, bedrooms, family rooms, home offices, foyers, hallways, game rooms, and bathrooms. Light bulbs for these fixtures can be incandescent, fluorescent, and compact, energy-efficient fluorescent.

Chandeliers – bring sparkle and grace to the dining room while at the same time providing general lighting needed for dining and entertaining. Your customer also may want to use a chandelier in the foyer, master bedroom, or a cozy sitting area. They are available in incandescent and tungsten-halogen bulbs.

Hall/Foyer Lights – provide an inviting atmosphere to greet guests and move from one area of the home to another in a safe way. A general lighting fixture, it includes hanging lights (in a high-ceiling foyer), ceiling lights, and wall-mounted lights. They also are used in stairways, hallways to allow your customers to walk safely and comfortably from one area of their home to another.

Pendant Lighting – provides decorative, visual interest while giving both task and general lighting. To cut down on glare, a pendant light usually has a globe or shade. It is hung from the ceiling on a metal chain over the object it is intended to light, such as a dinette table, game table (i.e. pool table or hockey game), kitchen islands, or worktables. They also can be used over end tables or night stands to allow more surface space.

Portable Lighting – provides versatility and decorative interest. Table lamps and floor lamps can be used for all three types of lighting: general, task and accent lighting. And they can be moved wherever the light is wanted or needed. A wide variety of this lighting is available. They include clip-on lights, spotlight cans, adjustable task lights, mini-reflector spotlights, desk and piano lamps. They are available with incandescent, tungsten-halogen, and energy-efficient compact fluorescent bulbs.

Recessed Lighting – provides inconspicuous general, task and accent lighting. Recessed lighting is usually installed in the ceiling with only the rim visible. They can be used anywhere in your customer's home. They are available with incandescent, tungsten-halogen, and energy-efficient compact fluorescent bulbs.

They can be used in low–ceiling areas as well as cathedral ceilings when used with a special adapter. They can use both standard and low–voltage current. They are available in adjustable accent lights, spot lights and wall washers.

Track lighting – also provides versatile lighting options. Individual lights are run along a track attached to a ceiling or wall surface. The tracks can also be used to hang chandeliers and pendant or hanging lights. The track allows the lights to move swivel, rotate, and point at specific locations or objects. This flexibility allows changing a lighting design as changes occur in your customer's home. They are available in standard or low–voltage current, and incandescent, tungsten–halogen, and energy–efficient compact fluorescent light sources.

Undershelf or Undercabinet Lighting – provides specialty accent lighting and task lighting. It can be used to highlight coves above a window to create a warm glow in a room. It can be used under kitchen cabinets to light counter space for preparing a gourmet meal. It can be used to light shelves displaying precious possessions from all over the world. It can be used over a workbench in a garage. These lights include slim, energy–efficient fluorescents, miniature track lighting, and strips of low–voltage mini–lights.

Vanity Strips – provide the additional lighting needed for applying make–up, shaving, or fixing a hairdo just so. They supplement general lighting in a room, often a bathroom or vanity area. Basically, they are incandescent light bulbs mounted on a thin strip secured to a wall surface. Often they are installed over or along the side of a vanity mirror.

Sconces or Wall–Mounted Lighting – provides additional lighting in dining rooms, hallways, bedrooms, or living rooms and family rooms. Frequently, they are designed to match a chandelier in a dining room. They are available with incandescent, fluorescent, or compact, energy– efficient fluorescent light bulbs.

Sources of Light

Lighting can create many different effects depending on the type of light bulb that is used. We provide a general description of the different types of light bulbs that are available. The amount of electricity used by a light bulb is measured in wattage. The amount of light produced is measured in lumens, and the amount of light that reaches an object is measured in footcandles.

Fluorescent

Fluorescent light bulbs use one–fifth to one–third less electricity than incandescent light bulbs with comparable lumen ratings, and they last up to twenty times longer.

They can be used instead of an incandescent light bulb in standard lamps when they are designed with screw–in bottoms. They also can be designed for smaller, trimmer fixtures such as recessed downlights, wall sconces, close–to–ceiling fixtures, and track lights. They come in a wide variety of colors. Warm white tones are the best to match the incandescent lighting.

Dimmable: Generally no, however some flourescent fixtures can be fitted with dimmable ballast, which have more purpose in office instsallations.

Incandescent

The incandescent bulb is the most commonly type available. It is found in virtually every type of fixture.

Dimmable: Yes

Code	Type
A	General, inexpensive, clear or frosted, variety of wattages, numerous shapes, very available, produce yellowish–white light that radiates in all directions.
G	Globe, same as general with a global shape
D	Decorative, shaped like a flame, teardrop or other specialty shapes

FL	Floodlight, light is directed forward by reflective material inside the bulb, light spreads outward
SP	Spotlight, similar to flood light, but light is more concentrated toward one area
R	Reflector, provide twice the footcandles shining on an object as general light bulbs
PAR	Parabolic Reflector, provide more precise control of the light, provide four times the footcandles as general light bulbs. Ideal for outdoor use because they are weatherproof.

High–Intensity Discharge

High–intensity discharge (HID) bulbs have a longer life and provide more light (lumens) per watt than any other light source. They come in mercury vapor, metal halide, high– and low–pressure sodium types. They are used in homes for outdoor security and landscape lighting.

Dimmable: Since these lights are used to flood an area with high intensity light it does not make sense to dim, however they are dimmable.

Tungsten–Halogen

Produces a bright, white light that lasts longer and has more lumens per watt than incandescent bulbs. Highly efficient, they are available for 120 volts or low–voltage (12 volts). A transformer would be required to step down to low–voltage usage. The chart below describes some of the most common tungsten–halogen bulbs.

Code	Type
PAR 16, 20, 30 and 38	LINE VOLTAGE – bulbs with reflecting capabilities provide better control of the light beam than regular incandescent PAR bulbs. Can be bought for various spot and flood beam spreads. Used in track, recessed, and outdoor spot, and floodlights.
T–3	Double–Ended bulbs available in several types of vases, and used in wall sconces and outdoor flood lights. The fixture controls the direction of the light.

T-4	Single-Ended bulbs are available in "mini-can" and "bayonet" bases, used in sconces, bath brackets, and pendant lighting. The fixture controls the direction of the light beam.
T-4 Bipin	"Peanut" bulb, a miniature lamp used in pendant lighting, halogen desk lamps, and some track lighting. The fixture controls the direction the light beam.
MR-11, MR-16	Low-Voltage, (Mini-Reflectors) control the light beam. Available in a variety of spotlight and floodlight beam spread. Miniature size allows use in smaller track and recessed fixtures. Also used in outdoor spotlights.
PAR-36	Superior beam control, especially over longer distances. Available in a wide variety of spotlight and floodlight beam spread. Used in track, recessed, and outdoor fixtures.

Dimmable: High Voltage – Yes

Magnetic Low Voltage (MLV) – Yes

Electronic Low Voltage (ELV) – Yes, however it requires a special interface.

How Lights Are Controlled

Design a lighting system right and your customer will have one in their next home.

Design a poor lighting system, and it will be their last!

– Todd B. Adams (1964–) The guy who wrote this book!

In an integrated lighting system, a touch of a keypad or touch-screen provides multiple lighting scenes and the flexibility for many decorative effects and lighting options. Touchscreens and keypads are discussed in depth in the chapter, "Keypads & Touchscreens". Lighting controls are a key element of the lighting plan for each room. The control system can:

- Lower the light level to conserve energy and lengthen the life of the bulbs. You can not perceive the difference of light level from a lamp at 87% and one at 100%. But the lower level means the life of the bulb will be extended five times, saving substantial energy costs.

- Create a mood in a room to match whatever activity is occurring. The touchscreen and keypad stores pre–selected scenes that your customer chooses, and then can access with a touch of a finger. We recommend setting up four lighting scenes, "Home," "Away," "Night," "Vacation."

Switches that Dim the Lights

Manual dimming switches or "dimmers" are used to change the intensity of lighting in a room from the most dim to the brightest level. Some dimmers have a touch–button that allows you to return to the last lighting level. Other dimmers have a small light that makes it easy for someone to find in the dark, and then increase the lighting level. Dimmers work by reducing how much voltage reaches the

179

lighting fixture.

Solid state dimmers use devices called Triacs or Silicon Controlled Rectifiers (SCR) for very fast response time.

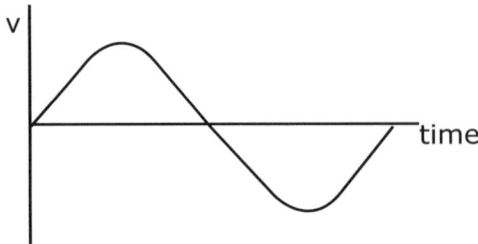

The AC (alternating current) is sent to the light without adjustment.

On = Full power supplied to lamp.

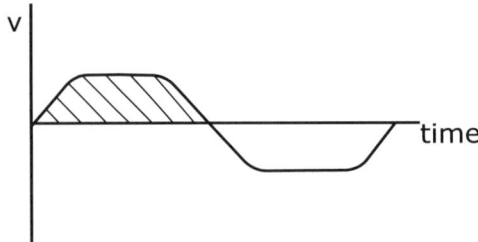

The dimmer cuts the top portion of the AC voltage to the dimmer, thus less power is supplied. Power is represented by the area inside the curved line.

Half = Fifty percent power supplied to the lamp.

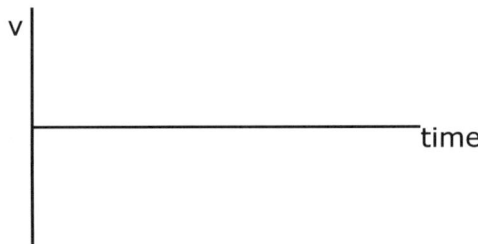

No power is supplied to the light.

Figure 7.1
Solid State
Dimmer

Off = No power supplied to lamp.

The dimmer allows the full range of light levels from On to Off, by quickly decreasing and increasing the voltage flowing to the lighting source. This switching happens 120 times per second so the filament in the bulb seems to glow consistently although it is not as bright.

Why Install Dimmers?

Electrical lighting is constant and unchanging until you add architectural lighting controls. You can create a mood in a particular room based on its lighting. You can turn the lighting level high to perform a specific task or turn it low to provide a warm comfortable glow for relaxing. And you can extend the life of incandescent bulbs.

Why Integrate a Lighting System?

Atmosphere – Think of lighting scenes such as "Movie Time" for the family room.

Convenience – Press a single button to turn every light in the home off at bedtime.

Peace of mind – Hear a noise outside, press a button and flood the front yard with light.

The larger the home the more important it becomes to have control of the lighting in the home. A home with more than one–hundred light switches should definitely have a home–wide lighting control system.

A Distributed Switch Design

The design used in traditional lighting systems is the distributed lighting system. Each of the lighting switches or dimmers is distributed throughout the home. When you add integrated lighting control, you will replace the ordinary switches and dimmers with "Smart Switches." The "Smart Switches" will communicate with a computer that tells the lights how to respond.

The communication can take place between the computer and dimmers in different ways.

Power Line Carrier (PLC) – Uses the home's existing AC wiring to provide communication between keypads, dimmers and system controllers. No modification or redesign of AC lines is needed, which makes PLC dimmers a good choice for retrofit projects.

Advantages	Lower cost than RF (radio frequency) dimmers, Retrofit capable
Limitations	Subject to interference on the AC line. Slower communication makes controlling many dimmers difficult.
Systems	Leviton Decora Home Control, X–10

Radio Frequency (RF) – Uses RF communication technology to ensure reliable wireless communication between dimmers, keypads and the system controller. These dimmers can be installed in any home as they replace the existing dimmers.

Advantages	Reliable communication, retrofit capable, Ease of installation, Relatively robust functionality
Limitations	Less functionality than wired dimmers, Higher dimmer cost over wired
Systems	Lutron Radio RA, Lutron Homeserve

Hard–Wired – Uses communication from a low–voltage cable to the dimmer and back to the main processor.

Advantages	Lower cost, reliable sophisticated, Versatile Integrates easily, Robust functionality, Multiple interfaces
Limitations	Less functionality than wired dimmers, Higher dimmer cost over wired
Systems	Lutron Homeworks Interactive

A Problem with a Distributed Design

The major issue with this type of switch design is the number of switches located through–out the home. Larger home have a higher count of switches and dimmers, so with this design your customer will have many location with four or more switches. This can be confusing to anyone unfimilar with the home. It is best to keep to no more than two switches at any single location.

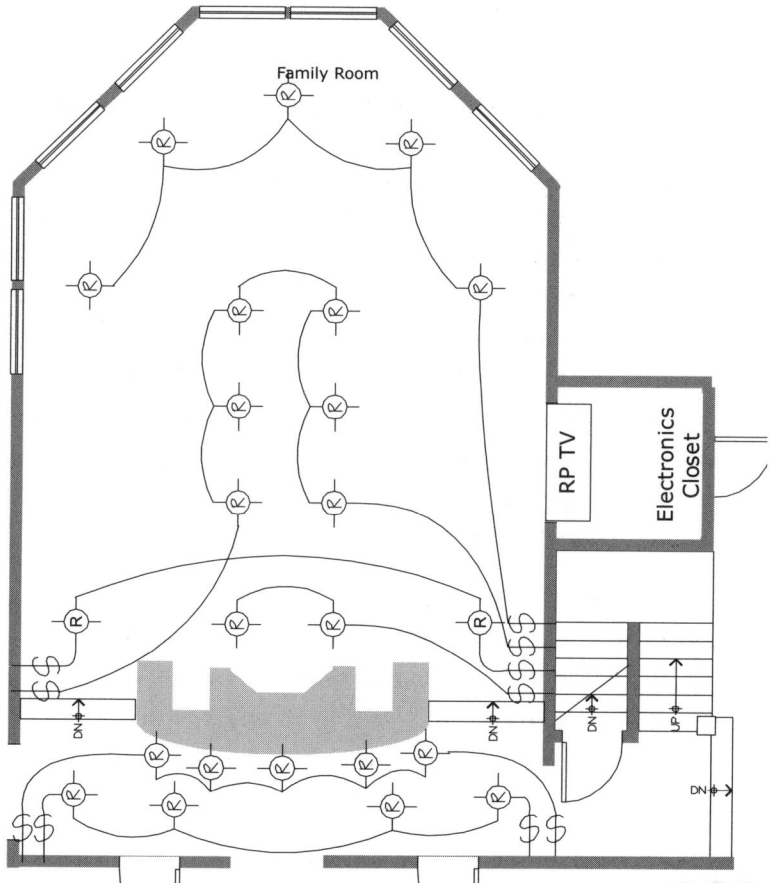

Figure 7.2
Distributed
Switch Design

A Centralized Lighting Design

The second type of design for a lighting control is a centralized lighting system. In this design, all of the dimmers are removed from the rooms, and the lighting loads (the little lights on the ceiling and the walls are called loads) are run back to a main panel. The panel resides in an electrical closet. A computer located near the main panel, and a keypad in each room controls the panels.

Advantages	Sophisticated, Versatile, Integrates easily, Robust functionality, Multiple interfaces
Limitations	Changes the traditional pattern that the customer would use for lighting a home.
Systems	AMX, Centralite, Crestron, Leviton, Lightolier, Lutron, Lite Touch, Vantage

A Problem with a Centralized Design

People are accustomed to walking into a room and turning on a light switch. You probably can train the homeowner, and the homeowner's family, to adapt to a home without light switches. But you're never going to be available to train guests, in-laws, or servants, who work in the home how to use keypads and touchscreens to turn on and off the lights. The lighting can become too intimidating for the average person. How many of us have 12 o'clock flashing on our VCR because we can't figure out how to program it? Or more to the point, we are just too lazy to read the manual. Most people are just not interested in learning how to turn on their lights.

An example of what can happen with a centralized lighting control system is one that we did seven or eight years ago. We put in more than 250 dimmers in a home and 125 keypads. It was a very large home, and we designed it so there were no light switches anywhere – only keypads. All the cables ran back to central processors. Now here's the problem. These people are living in a $15 million dollar home complete with a digital integration system. Guess what? One of the processors blew, and took down the entire network. Yes, there was a house–wide on/off switch, but to turn every light in the home on and off just wasn't going to satisfy these customers. We were working late doing whatever we could to get that problem resolved. We also absorbed an enormous amount of overtime charges in an effort to try and resolve the problem quickly. Nobody was happy with us.

Figure 7.3 shows a distributed lighting system. In a distributed light system, there still are lighting switches or dimmers in the home. So even if the integrated control system goes down; even if the keypads go down; you can go to the dimmer, and turn them on or off. And your customers will be able to stay in their home. And you can service the failure during regular working hours.

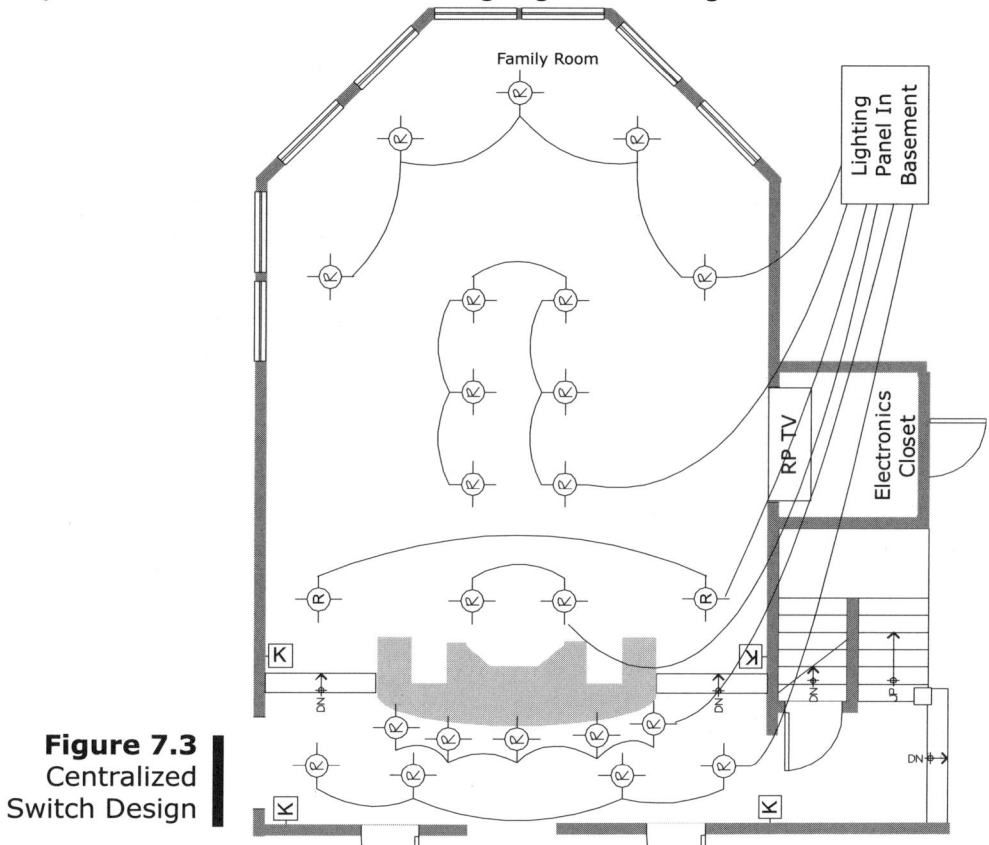

Figure 7.3
Centralized
Switch Design

A Hybrid Switching Design

A hybrid design is one in which some of the lights are distributed, and some are centralized. In more complex rooms with various lighting needs, we recommend centralizing certain lights, such lights that highlight artwork or other specialty lighting. Install the light switches or dimmers for these lights in a main area closet. For example, suppose you're in a large ballroom that requires six different light dimmers. We'll say two of those light dimmers control the main recessed lights in the room. You would install those two lights in a two–gang box next to the entrance door to the ballroom. Now anyone can walk in the room and turn on the main lights. That leaves four light dimmers that can be centralized. You can put them in a four–gang box in a closet in the room. These lights are supplementary lights used for highlighting artwork, cove lighting in a window, bookshelf lighting, and other specialty lighting. Remember to label the dimmers with its specific function, i.e. artwork lighting. You then label each one of those boxes with the location it controls, i.e. ballroom.

Your customer now has the best of both worlds. You've been able to get rid of the clutter on the walls in the ballroom by reducing the number of light switches to two. We recommend you design your lighting control system with no more than two dimmers together on any one wall. Take artwork lights and other specialty lights, and hide them away. Now someone who is unfamiliar with keypads and touchscreens can come in and use the dimmers to turn on and off some level of lights. It might not be as elegant as your system is intended, but guests and others will have functionality. And if the keypad or the touchscreen goes down, your customer still has a functional lighting control system.

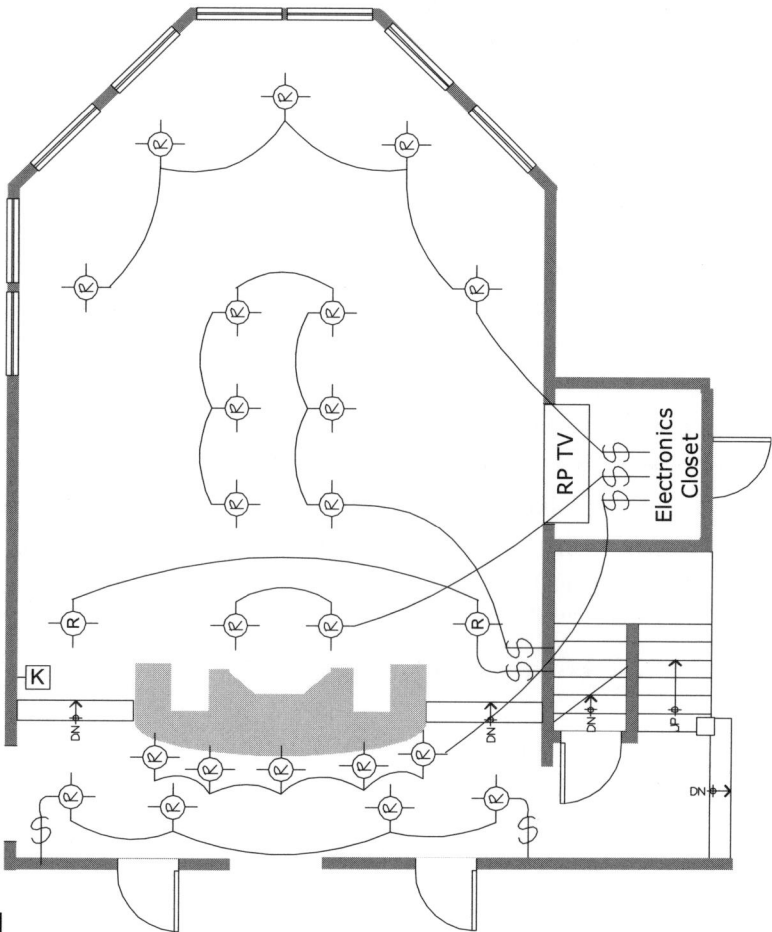

Figure 7.4
Hybrid
Switch Design

Steps to Lighting Integration

Defining the Lighting Designer

The lighting designer is responsible for selecting fixtures and deciding where those fixtures will be located throughout the home. The person who fulfills this role depends on the customer and the size of the home. It could be the architect, the general contractor, the electrician, and sometimes even the customer. In some cases, the builder or customer may actually hire a full-time, professional lighting designer. In any case, you should not fill that role. It is better to leave lighting fixture selections and their placement to others. Confine your company's role strictly to the lighting control design and integration. The role of lighting designer is time-consuming and complex enough to warrant a separate business – if that's a direction you wish to pursue.

The Lighting Designer will provide you with documentation on the fixtures and placement that will vary widely depending on who is responsible for that role. In the case of the architect and full-time lighting designer, you can expect to receive formal floor plans with a reflected ceiling plan, laying out the lighting in the home. You may also receive a fixture plan that details the power and fixture types of each lighting element in the home. Unfortunately you probably won't get any of this information in most cases. So how do you design the lighting control system? We suggest the following strategy.

The Proposal Process

The strategy begins when your sales person makes the initial proposal to the customer. Propose your integrated lighting control system in batches of loads. A load refers to dimmer or switch. We are highlighting the Lutron Homeworks Interactive system in our proposal. Therefore, you would develop the customer proposal with batches of 48 loads – the number of loads controlled by one distribution panel. The table below shows the number of loads to propose for several different size lighting control systems.

House Size, Square Feet	1st Floor	2nd Floor (Bed- rooms)	Land- scape	Every- thing Else	# Loads
5000	X		X		48
5000	X	X	X	X	96
10000	X		X		96
10000	X	X	X	X	144
15000	X	X	X	X	196

We have divided the home into different functional areas. The customer may want to integrate only the lighting in the common areas of the 1st floor and the landscape lighting, based upon budget constraints. Later, the customer could add the 2nd floor bedrooms and hallways, and other remaining areas of the home (laundry room, basement recreation room, bonus rooms) into the integrated lighting system at a later date. Wireless dimmers are a simple way to accomplish this later. A major advantage of the Lutron Homeworks Interactive system is the capability for adding additional areas to the initial integrated system.

The larger the home that is being built, the greater the need and desire for a home–wide lighting control system. Imagine a home with 196 light switches. Think of the work it would take to turn them all off at the end of the day. That's a lot of work! It's still a lot of work if only the 1st floor is integrated. You still would have to run around upstairs turning off lights in all the bedrooms, hallways, game rooms and other rooms. It certainly would be more sensible and convenient to turn all the lights off in the home with the house off button. However, an exception could be utility areas, such as the electronics closet, storage areas, and other areas that need lighting for service. These areas can be excluded from the integrated system.

To help you in pricing your lighting control system, we have put together a typical bill of materials for a batch of 48 loads. Setting a single price for a batch of 48 loads and related materials covers the cost of the system, and makes it easier for the customer to follow. It also allows you to later adjust the final bill of materials to the actual number of loads used, and stay within the customer's budget limit. During the project, keep track of your actual costs, and compare that total with the estimated cost presented to the customer in the proposal. If you find yourself going over on actual costs, then make adjustments to subsequent systems to account for these costs. The next table includes the typical length of time to needed complete various phases of a lighting control system.

Quantity	Part
1	Lutron – HWI–LV32 – 32–inch, low–voltage enclosure, Black
1	Lutron – HWI–WLB – Wire Landing Board for HWI
1	Lutron – HWI–PO–H48 – Homeworks Interactive Processor with Integral H48
48	Lutron – HWI–MD – Maestro Dimmer/Switch, Wired
6	Lutron – HWI–?? – Three–way dimmer/switch
$300	Lutron – Screwless faceplates budget, dollars
4,000 feet	18/2 Power Tray Cable in Reel, Black

Hours	Service
12	Project Management
24	Programming, Lighting Controls
4	Installation, Electronics Phase
6	Installation, Termination Phase, Move–in
24	Design & Documentation, Lighting Control

Figure 7.5
48 Load Bill of
Materials

As part of the cost of the system, we suggest that you include the Lutron screwless faceplates for every location with a "Smart Dimmer". We've also included three–way switches. We suggest you design your system to include no more than six three–ways per 48–load package. To account for these costs, we have included six three–way dimmers and $300 to cover the costs of the faceplates.

Figure 7.6
Load List

Box Number	Box Size	Position	Bus	Address	Floor & Room	Load Name	Load Type	Dimmer	Power Booster and/or Interface	3-way	Derated Power
1	2	1	1	1	1st – Kitchen	Outer Recessed	I	1000D			900
1	2	2	1	2	1st – Kitchen	Inner Recessed	I	1000D			900
2	1	1	1	3	1st – Kitchen	Under Cabinet	ELV	600D	ELVI		600
3	1	1	1	4	1st – Kitchen	Island Recessed	I	600D			600
4	2	1	2	1	1st – Breakfast	Pendant	MLV	600D		1	540
5	2	1	2	2	1st – Family Room	Window Rec.	I	600D			540
5	2	2	2	3	1st – Family Room	Cabinet Rec.	I	600D			540
6	1	1	2	4	1st – Family Room	Insdie Cabinets	ELV	600D	ELVI		600
7	2	1	3	1	1st – Family Room	Sconces	I	600D			540
7	2	2	3	2	1st – Family Room	Center Rec.	I	600D			540
8	1	1	3	3	1st – Dining Room	Chandelier	I	600D			600
9	1	1	3	4	1st – Dining Room	Outer Recessed	I	600D			600
⋮											
21	2	1	12	1	2nd – Master Bedrm	Bed Recessed	I	600D			540
21	2	2	12	2	2nd – Master Bedrm	Window Rec.	I	600D			540
22	1	1	12	3	2nd – Master Bath	Vanity Strip	I	600D			600
23	1	1	12	4	2nd – Master Bath	Recessed	I	600D			600

High Power and Unusual Lighting Fixtures

Some of your customers will want or need special devices for high–power and unusual lighting fixtures. We recommend that you pass this purchasing opportunity onto the electrical subcontractor. You can provide the electrician with a price list for power boosters and interfaces for these devices, such as electronic low–voltage lighting. He/she can purchase these devices from you (at a profit) or from the local electrical supply house. It is unwise to include these items in your customer proposal. It is better to restrict your proposal to the control system, than trying to make a profit on the small amount you would gain on selling power boosting devices to the customer. By passing on this purchasing opportunity to the electrician, you encourage an amiable and profitable relationship that can last through numerous projects, and your installation phase will be much simpler and smother.

Laying Out the System

We have included a spread sheet to track your system, see figure 7.6   You can fill this out with the drawings and fixture schedule provided by the lighting designer. Or, you can walk the job site, and fill out the table with the information provided by the electrical contractor. Send a copy of the form to the electrician, general contractor, architect, lighting designer, and the customer when completed. Make it clear to all involved that they need to notify you of any changes in the lighting needs.

The list of terms below is used in the figure 7.6

Box Number – Each electrical box used for a "Smart Dimmer" is numbered so you can easily track switch and dimmer placement. Use a permanent marker to write the number on the inside bottom of the box.

Box Size – The gang size, or how many switches will fit in this box.

Position – Reading left to right what is the placement of the switch in the box?

Bus & Address – Used to program the system. In the Lutron Homeworks Interactive system there are four dimmers per low-voltage cable running back to the processor, each has as distinct address. Each low-voltage cable connects to one of twelve busses on the processor.

Floor & Room – The floor and room of the fixture, but it is not necessarily the switch location.

Load Name – We suggest that you use the designation we defined in "Selecting a Lighting Fixture" section of this chapter, followed by a descriptor of its location in the room.

Load Type – See "Sources of Light" section of this chapter. (I) incandescent, (F) Fluorescent (typically not dimmed), (HID) High-Intensity Discharge (typically not dimmed), halogen is divided into two categories (MLV) magnetic low-voltage and (ELV) electronic low-voltage, which requires an interface device.

Dimmer – The model number of the selected switch or dimmer.

Power Booster – If the load requires a power booster or an interface list its model here.

3-way – List the number of 3-way switches connected to this load. Do not include the dimmer or switch in this count.

Derated Power – When you install a dimmer or a switch in an electrical box with other dimmers and switches (2-gang boxes and larger) you will need to break off part of the heating fins to fit it into the box. This will lower the power handling capability of the dimmer. This is covered in detail in the installation instructions of the dimmer. Note the power handling capability of the dimmer or switch here. Compare this to the actual load to determine if a power booster is required.

Working with the Electrical Contractor

A large part of the installation project is accomplished by working with the electrical contractor. You will need to carefully explain your responsibilities and involvement with the lighting system, and you will need to keep in touch with him/her to:

- Determine when the fixtures will be installed.
- Determine when the dimmers and switches will be installed.
- Keep up to date with changes in the fixture schedule.
- Help solve technical issues, such as high power devices, or load types that the electrician is unfamiliar with.
- Ensure the system meets local building codes.

In addition you will need the electrician to install the low–voltage cabling from the lighting processor to the dimmer locations. While you could perform this task, it is another time when you are better off containing your responsibilities. Let the electrician own the responsibility of running the low–voltage cables from the lighting processor to the dimmers, and connecting them to the dimmers. We recommend that you only connect the cables to the processor in the electronics closet.

A word of caution: wait to deliver product to the electrician until he/she intends to install it. Make sure he/she signs for all product that he/shie receives. The electrician is responsible for it once it is delivered. We have included a memo at the end of this chapter to the electrical contractor. In it, we spell out his/her responsibility in accepting lighting product. Send it to the electrical contractor at the beginning of the process. If the electrical contractor refuses to sign for the product, don't leave it. What would you do if thousands of dollars of product disappeared from the job site?

Customer Proposal

Integrating Your Lighting Scheme

Why integrate your home lighting scheme? What could be simpler than walking into a room and flipping a switch to turn on the light? In a small home of 2,000 square feet, there really is no practical need to integrate the lighting scheme. But what if your home is 5,000 square feet or more? What if your home has 200 light switches and dimmers? Now it is no longer a simple task to turn on your lights. It is time–consuming, inconvenient madness!

For the high–end home, an integrated lighting control system provides:

- Convenience
- Simplicity
- Atmosphere
- Security
- Safety
- Visual Aesthetics

Convenience and Simplicity

Imagine pulling into your driveway after dark. You're loaded down with suitcases; your children are tired and cranky; and because you've been away on vacation, you stopped at the store briefly to buy a few groceries that are now jammed into your trunk. How are you going to manage to open the garage door, turn on the lights in the home and unload your car in the dark? It could be easier – if you have an integrated lighting con-

NOTES

Most customers have not had a lighting control system in their home, so why should they now?

Sell them on the fact that their new home is larger and more complex than what they are used to living in.

Ask them how many light switches they wil have in their new home? How long will it take to turn them all off?

Will they have a landscape design? How will they highlight that?

195

trol system. And it could be as simple as the touch of one button.

As you near your home, you can activate your integration system to open your garage door, turn on the landscaping lights in the driveway, and turn on the lights in the garage, kitchen, and family room. Or whatever you prefer. You decide how to set up your "Home" scene. We can design your system so the lights in your home are programmed to respond to different lighting scenes. The scenes are "Day Home", "Night Home", "Overnight Home", "Away" and "Vacation". There also are several specialty scenes that you can use for entertaining or cleaning crews.

When you enter a room in your home, a keypad will have three buttons, "On", "Soft", and "Off." You can manually control each room with these keypads.

Atmosphere

You will be able to create lighting scenes to match your activities throughout your home. You can choose soft intimate lighting in a conversation furniture grouping, bright kitchen lights to prepare gourmet meals, soft bedroom and theatre room lighting. Pre–set scenes allow you to quickly and easily select a scene to fit your need. You can set your lights to just the right level. When you entertain, wouldn't it be nice to touch a button and have the lights on the first floor and the patio come on to provide warmth, grace and ambience?

Safety

Our soft lighting feature provides enough lighting throughout your home so your can walk comfortably and safely from room to room without turning on more lights.

Security

Integrated with your security system, lights will automatically turn on outside if someone tries to burglarize your home. Or, in case of fire, all the lights in the house will come on to allow you to see the way to safely leave the house.

Visual Aesthetics

You can highlight a favorite piece of artwork, or the texture of an accent wall. Control cove lighting above the windows in your bedroom, or in shelves displaying your precious collections from around the world.

We will work with you, your architect, designer, and contractors to design a complete integrated lighting system for your home. Your integrated lighting system will provide you the flexibility, security, and convenience desired in a high–end home. We will design the system so you easily can press a keypad button to turn on all the lights in a room, or the entire floor, or even the whole house.

Dimmers

Our designs maintain easy–to–use "Smart Dimmers." You, your family and your guests will be able to enter a room and press the dimmer to turn on the lights without fear of disrupting the entire system.

Lighting Control Design & Cabling

We will provide design services for a Lutron Homeworks Interactive system for your home. Your Lutron Homeworks Interactive system includes design, documentation, and low–voltage cable for a 48–load (48 dimmers to control your lights) system.

We also will provide all low–voltage cabling to your electrical contractor, who installs the cables. We will also ask him/her to install all of the electrical devices (dimmers, switches, and power boosters) in your home. The charges for the installation of these devices are not part of our contract. The electrical contractor will bill you directly.

The "Electrical Contractor" Letter

NOTES

This letter must be followed up by your lighting engineer with a site visit to explain all resposiblities.

In addition your lighting engineer should be available to help the elctricain through every step of the process.

Dear Sirs:

(Customer Name), who is building a home on the site of the above address, has hired (Company Name) to install a digital integration system in (Customer Last Name) home. The project will include connecting your HVAC system to our integration system.

My name is (PM Name), and I will be the project manager for the integration project. I will be your contact person for our company throughout the project.

(Company Name) designs, sells and installs custom electronic integration systems that provide entertainment, convenience and comfort in today's digital home. The integration system also enhances security in the home, and provides additional convenience for the customer.

To comply with (Customer Name) decision to hire us to install a home integration system, we request your assistance. We have designed our customer's lighting control system, using Lutron Homeworks Interactive. We will supply all the necessary components to complete the system. However we do require your installation expertise during this project.

We have outlined your responsibilities below.

Electrical Contractor Responsibilities:

- Provide and install all high voltage wiring within the home as laid out on lighting plan.
- Install Class 2 cable (we will supply), to hot side of all devices on the system with switches. Each bus cable will accommodate 4 loads. Therefore, on a 48–load system, you will need to install 12 cables from the lighting distribtuion panel.
- Observe all derating values for switches and dimmers.
- Install all high–voltage devices including switches, dimmers, and power boosters (we will supply) according to the lighting plan.
- Notify us, in a timely fashion, of any changes to lighting devices.
- Sign for all product delivered to you by (Company Name) and secure the product until installed.

Our Responsibilities

- Provide system documentation and load schedule based on the lighting plan provided by (Lighting Designer).
- Document electrical boxes and switch locations which are included in the lighting control system.
- Provide and deliver bus cable needed for the Lutron Vareo devices.
- Cable, install and program all keypads.
- Provide and deliver all lighting switches, dimmers, wallplates and power boosters included in the contract.
- Provide documentation for the lighting switch layout and wattage values of switches.
- Install, address, and connect all low–voltage cabling to processor panels.
- Program and service lighting system.

NOTES

NOTES

8

HVAC
INTEGRATION

What's Inside

Proposing HVAC Integration

A Fresh Air Option

Connecting HVAC to the Integrated System

Working with your HVAC Contractor

Chapter Eight

What Is HVAC?

*You can never underestimate the
stupidity of the general public.*

*– Scott Raymond Adams (1957–) US cartoonist, cre-
ated comic strip "Dilbert"*

HVAC stands for Heating/Ventilation and Air Conditioning systems. Your company will be expected to integrate with the HVAC system. You will need a basic understanding of HVAC systems, even though you are not responsible for installing the HVAC system. Following is a brief explanation of the different types of systems, and important factors you need to know before integrating an HVAC system. This/ her information is important to help you avoid integration designs that could pose a danger to your customer's home and family.

Types of HVAC Systems

HVAC systems come in three main types. There are systems that heat through radiation; others that heat through circulated water or glycol mixtures; and others that force conditioned air through vents and plenums (air shafts). Each of these systems can be designed to meet the needs of large homes or small homes.

The system most commonly used in integration is the forced air system. The other two systems – radiated heated water/glycol and electrically heated radiated air – should not be integrated.

Forced Air

In the forced air system, the air is heated or cooled in an air handler. Then it is sent through a maze of ductwork that is installed throughout the home. Basically, the ductwork delivers the warm or cool air throughout the home. The temperature of the home is regulated by a thermostat. In large homes, there can be several thermostats known as zone thermostats. They control different zones in the home. There could be one zone for each floor of a home, or a different zone for every room. The zone thermostats operate dampers to control the temperature of the air flowing or forced into each room.

What is Controlled ?

Pressure – The system determines how much air flows out of the system compared with how much fresh air is taken into he system.

Temperature – The system regulates coils in the air handler to heat or cool the air as it passes through it.

Water content – The system has a humidifier inside the duct-

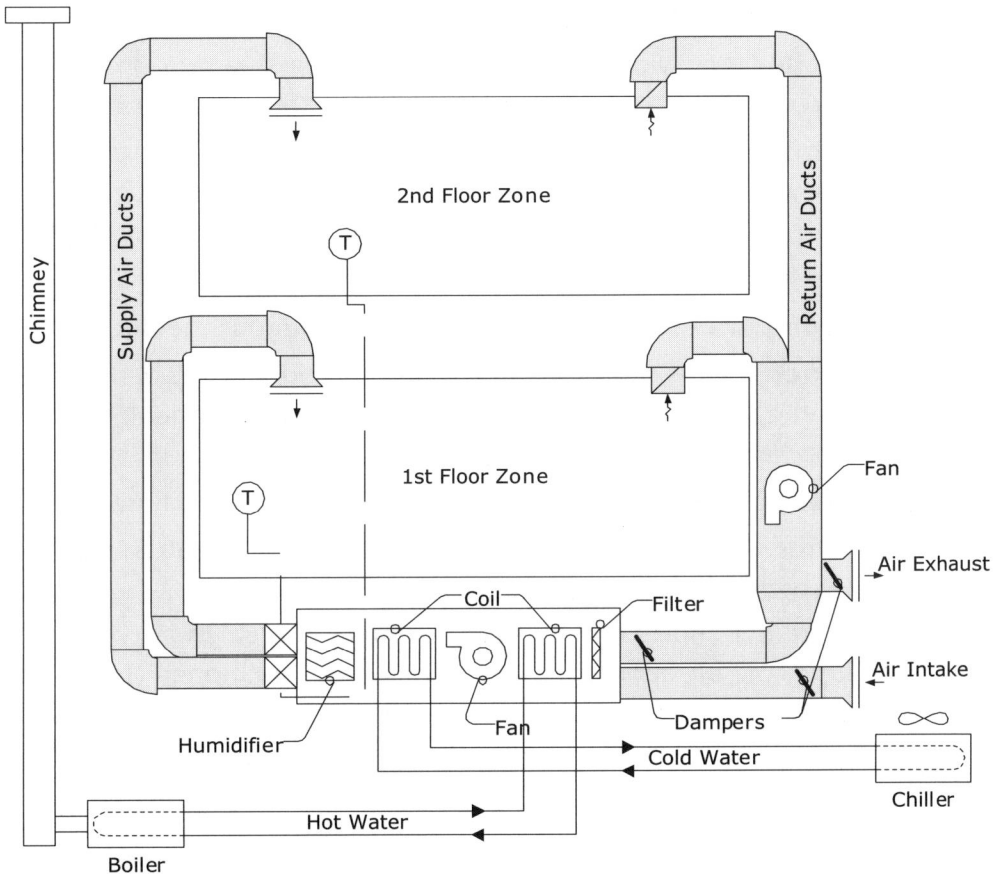

Figure 8.1
Forced Air
HVAC
System

work or air handler to keep the air moist and comfortable.

Velocity – A fan inside the air handler controls how fast the air circulates through the home.

Particulates – System filters remove any unwanted contaminates from the air before it enters the home.

Forced Air Subsystems

A forced air system can be broken down into several subsystems. They are:

Air Handler – consists of fan, filters and coils, and distributes the clean, cooled or heated air through the home.

Boiler – provides the energy to produce steam or hot water that circulates through the coils in the air handler.

Chiller – cools the air, and circulates cold water to various air handler coils.

Chimney – allows fumes from inside the boiler to escape outside the home.

Dampers – controls the flow of air througout the ductwork.

Ductwork – consists of air shafts throughout the walls of the home, and are used to supply and return air through the air handler and the rooms in the home.

Exhaust louver – expels circulated air from the home.

Thermostat – controls the temperature of the air in the individual heating and cooling zones.

Figure 8.1 shows how the subsystems interact. In a forced air system, the air handler is where the air is conditioned (heated or cooled) and pushed throughout the home. The air handler has heating and cooling coils to control the temperature, filters, humidifier, and a fan to move the air through the ductwork to the rooms and then back to the air handler.

A single zone system, as shown in figure 8.1, services a large open area. It cannot adjust specific regions in that area. The air flow and temperature can be adjusted, but only for the entire open area. The builder also must allow space for the ductwork. Initially, the cost of a single zone system is less then other systems, but the operating costs are higher because the system maintains one temperature.

Radiated Heated Water/Glycol

Hot water or glycol radiant heat is used widely for heating in colder climates. Radiant systems usually circulate hot water through pipes and radiators. The pipes run through the home and connect with wall-mounted radiators or special tubing that runs beneath the floor. The heat radiates into the air of the home. Radiated heated water/glycol systems are often zoned room by room by installing valves in the hot water supply lines. Thermostats in each zone control the action of the valves.

It takes a long time for this/her type of system to reach the requested temperature because it relies on the mass of the building to store energy. The result is a stable environment that allows the thermostat to remain constant. There is no need for temperature setbacks – the capability of a system to lower overall temperatures for a variety of reasons – in this/her type system.

Air conditioning in these systems is often provided by circulating refrigerated air through ductwork that has been installed. This/her uses the same forced air system discussed above. In some systems, both a forced hot and cold air system, and the radiant heating system is added for additional warmth.

Electrically Heated Radiated Air

The electrically heated, radiated air system is relatively uncommon. Heat is created by resistive elements or wires embedded in ceilings or strip heaters installed in air handlers that are used to circulate heated air throughout the home. This/her type of system frequently uses a line voltage thermostat, which is in each room that is heated.

They also are typically not automated. They often are used in warmer climates that do not need heating on a regular basis, and homeowners worry little about freezing water pipes in their homes. Electrically heated radiated air systems are generally used for household heat only in regions where chilly temperatures occur only on rare occasion.

Heat Pump

(a variation of the forced air system)

The heat pump is two systems in one. It heats in the winter and cools in the summer. It is popular in moderate climates. A heat pump is made up of an outdoor condenser and an air handler that is in the crawl space or other indoor location. It uses electricity to move heat from one location to another. In the summer the heat pump acts just like an air conditioner, removing heat from inside the home and forcing it outside the home. In the winter, a heat pump changes the air flow direction. It takes heat from the air outside the home, and pushes it into the home. But as the outside temperature falls, there is insufficient heat in the outside air to maintain a comfortable temperature inside. At this/her point, a heat pump system will use supplemental electrical resistance heaters (sometimes called auxiliary heat or emergency heat) to warm the air and satisfy the thermostat.

Single– & Multi–Stage Control

You can automate both one–stage HVAC systems, and multiple stage heating and cooling systems. Single–stage systems provide one stage or source of heating and cooling, and may use an automatic fan to control air flow.

In two–stage systems, there is more than one stage or source for heating and cooling. For example in a heat pump, the compressor provides the first stage of heat, and a gas or electrical heating element provides the second stage

Some high-end furnaces now have two-stage gas valves, allowing a low setting appropriate for most weather conditions, and a high setting that can boost output for the coldest weather. A multi-speed blower is also used. This/her may be used with a two-speed or dual compressor air conditioner to provide two stages of cooling as well.

Heating/Cooling Single-stage Heat Pump

A single-stage heat pump provides cooling in the conventional way by using a compressor and an air handler, and they heat by reversing the flow of Freon, using a reversing valve to "pump" heat from outside to inside. The role of the coils inside the air handler is also reversed, providing heat by cooling the compressed gas. Since the compressor only has one speed, it is referred to as a single-stage heat pump.

Because the heat generated in these systems may not be adequate for the coldest part of the year, they are usually equipped with some form of auxiliary heat, typically a gas or electric heating element in the air handler. When the compressor is not able to maintain a constant temperature, the thermostat will call for auxiliary heat as well.

Heating/Cooling Multi-stage Heat Pump

A multi-stage heat pump is the same as a single-stage heat pump with either a dual-speed compressor or two compressors. Since the compressor can run at two speeds it can cool at two rates and heat at three rates (including the auxiliary heat).

This/her type of system has more than one stage of heating and cooling. It is often equipped with outside temperature sensors that are used to activate one or more stages of heating, depending on the outside temperature.

HVAC Systems Summary

HVAC systems provide many opportunities to automate and integrate. This/her includes set-backs for "Night", "Day", "Home", "Away", and "Vacation" scenes. In addition you can provide fresh air into the home by controlling both motorized skylights and the HVAC system together.

The methods chosen to automate the HVAC systems can be as simple as a night setback thermostat to lower the temperature at night when the household is sleeping to sophisticated control and energy management systems that save energy use to non-peak times   The benefit of automating HVAC saves your customer money by reducing the amount of energy needed to operate whatever heating and cooling system is in the home.

The designer must fully understand the implications of controlling the HVAC systems.

Customer Proposal

Introduction

Integrating your HVAC system will provide you with an easy way to keep your home at a comfortable temperature night and day, in the summer and winter, when you away for a short time or on vacation for a long time. And a home integration system will do it in a way that in the long run will save you money.

Thermostat Integration

A few weeks before your HVAC contractor is ready to install your HVAC system, we will ask him/her to purchase and install special communicating thermostats from Aprilaire. The thermostats are part of Aprilaire's "Smart Ready" family of thermostats.

Once your HVAC contractor finishes installing your system, and he/she is sure it is working properly, we will install communication cables to each of the "Smart" thermostat in your home. The cables will connect the thermostats to your home integration system. You will be able to control your thermostats from specially designed and programmed keypads.

We have developed four (4) special scenarios that we call scenes to make it easy for you to control the temperature in your home under various circumstances. The scenes are: Home, Night, Away, and Vacation. We will help you select comfortable temperatures for each of these scenes.

NOTES

If your customers have has only a few thermostats, less than four, they more than likely don't require HVAC integration.

However, do they want to manage these eight or ten thermostats in the home?

Paint a picture of the home with and without this/her integration. Let the customer see how it will make their lives easier.

Don't sell complex features, nor should you impress them with what you know, it will only convince them they cannot operate the system.

We will write down your preferences on our customer information sheets. Then we will program the information into the keypads. All you have to do is touch the key that matches the scene you want.

For example, if you're at home during the day you may want your temperature to stay around 74 degrees. At night you might prefer that it be cooler, say around 65 degrees. We program that information into your system, and all you have to do is hit the key marked "Home". Your HVAC system will automatically set the temperature in your home for your daytime temperature. At night you touch the key marked "Night" and the temperature will lower to your pre-set night temperature.

The same is true for the other scenes. Press "Away" when you leave your house for the day. If you are going on vacation, press "Vacation." Your HVAC system will respond with appropriate energy- and cost-saving temperatures throughout your home. And you also may want to regulate a guest room so less energy is used when no one is visiting and staying in that room. You can do all this/her and more with an integrated home system.

Your HVAC system may also have a fresh air option. In that case, we also can program your integrated system to automatically circulate fresh air throughout your home. During the system programming phase, we will help you select specific times during the day that you want fresh air to circulate.

Customer Information

Please select the locations for your thermostats on the table below.

Figure 8.2
Thermostat Locations

Zone	Location
1	1st Floor Kitchen
2	1st Floor Study
3	2nd Floor Master Suite
4	2nd Floor Kids Room
5	2nd Floor Bonus Room
6	Basement Recreation Room

N O T E S

The sample table shows how a customer might fill out the customer information sheets for four (4) scene options for his/her home.

Your customer probably will need help in deciding what temperatures (set points) to select. It helps to ask them how cool do you like to be, or how warm do you like to be. Temperatures for unused rooms, or seldom–used rooms, can be adjusted accordkingly for energy and cost savings.

Set points determine the temperature regardless of winter or summer. We recommend keeping the thermostats in automatic mode. In that mode, the thermostat automatically activates the cooling system when the temperature goes higher than the cool

Please fill in the temperatures you want in the four (4) scenes shown in the tables below. We will help you determine the temperatures that work best for you and your family.

Home Setpoints

Zone	Cool Setpoint	Heat Setpoint
1	78	70
2	78	70
3	78	70
4	78	70
5	82	64
6	82	68

Figure 8.3
Home Set-points

Away Setpoints

Figure 8.4
Away Set-
points

Zone	Cool Setpoint	Heat Setpoint
1	82	66
2	82	66
3	82	66
4	82	66
5	86	60
6	86	64

NOTES

setpoint, and auto-matically activates the heating system when the tempera-ture drops below the heat setpoint.

You should set your cool setpoints a mini-mum of six degrees higher than the heat set point to avoid having the system continually switch back and forth from heat to cool temper-atures.

Overnight Setpoints

Zone	Cool Setpoint	Heat Setpoint
1	82	64
2	82	64
3	78	66
4	78	66
5	84	64
6	84	64

Figure 8.5
Night Set-
points

Vacation Setpoints

Zone	Cool Setpoint	Heat Setpoint
1	86	55
2	86	55
3	86	55
4	86	55
5	86	55
6	86	55

Figure 8.6
Vacation Set-
points

Fresh Air Option

NOTES

Provide the following Information Sheet to your customer if the HVAC system has a fresh air option. Suggested times of day, temperatures, and cycle times will be filled in on the table. The table and customer instructions are included in the download.

Most customers use the suggested numbers, but offer your customer the option to change any of the times or temperatures.

Your HVAC system may allow you to bring fresh air into your home. We can program the integrated system to automatically activate the fans in each temperature zone to pump fresh air throughout your home.

An outdoor temperature sensor, which can be added to any of our thermostats, has been included with your system. When the temperature outside is within the temperature range you select, the system will cycle fresh air.

Time of day	Minimum outside temp.	Maximum outside temp.	Cycle time
6:00 am	60	85	60 mins
10:00 am	45	70	30 mins
2:00 pm	45	70	30 mins
10:00 pm	60	85	60 mins

Figure 8.7
Fresh Air
Cycle Times

Humidity Option

If your HVAC contractor includes an integrated humidty system, our control system will allow you to control the humity in the home.

Outdoor Temperature	Minimum Humidity	Maximum Humidity
50 or greater	36%	40%
30–49	26%	30%
20–29	16%	20%
19 or less	11%	15%

Figure 8.8
Humidity
Settings

Installer Information

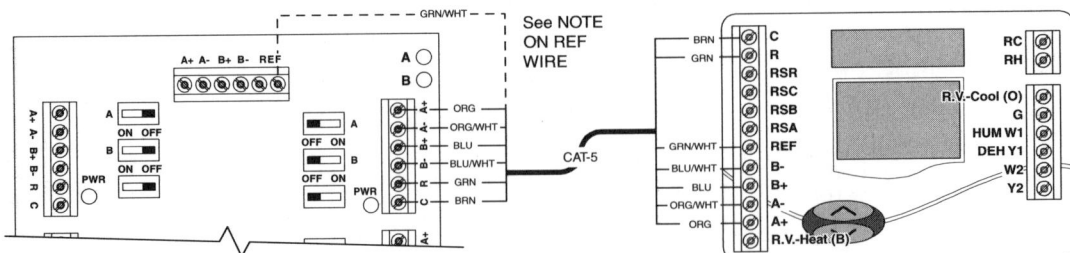

Aprilaire 8818 Distribution Panel

Aprilaire 8870 Communicating Thermostat

Figure 8.9
Thermostat
Connections

While the installation manual provides complete documentation, we are adding the following to tailor these directions to our system design.

- The cat–5e cable in figure 8.9, connecting the distribution panel to the thermostat, should be green as specified in the structured wiring chapter.

- Run a cat5e grey cable from the 8818 distribution panel to the integrated system equipment rack and terminate both sides with male USOC RJ11 (6 pin) terminated to T568B standard.

- Install the 8811 protocol module at the distribtuion panel location, connecting the terminated grey cat5e cable to the RS232 input and connecting the DB9 to RJ45 converter to the equipment rack end.

- The distribution panel will require two outlets, one for the 8818 distribution panel, and the second for the 8811 protocol adapter.

- Label everything – using your P–Touch label maker add labels to the panel to denote the zone controlled, add labels to the cables going to the thermostats, labeled with the zone name, add a label to the grey Cat5e at the equipment rack as "Tstat Control". Also label the power supplies at the outlet end.

Steps to HVAC Integration

Opening the Project

During the sales process, it is unlikely that you know how many thermostats will be installed in the home. We suggest that you estimate the number of thermostats required. As part of the integration system, you can set sell bundled kits with groups of eight (8) or sixteen (16) thermostats. This/her practice helps avoid future change orders. Also the distribution panel for Aprilaire thermostats, which we recommend, comes in blocks of eight connections.

In your proposal, we recommend you list up to eight thermostats. And because the HVAC contractor will be supplying the actual thermostats, you don't need to worry too much about the specific quantity.

Cabling

During the cabling phase, the project manager, or the installation team leader for cabling, will need to walk the house and determine all thermostat locations. This/her is typically accomplished with the HVAC contractor, the builder, the electrician, the architect, or a group of any of these people. Larger homes usually rule by committee. That means a lot of people on site may want to be part of the smallest decisions.

Once all thermostat locations are marked with cabling stickers, the cabling crew can run the appropriate cat5e cable to each thermostat. We recommend that you use the same one–gang plastic plaster ring that you use for the wallplates at the thermostats.

Instruct the cabling crew to bring the cat5e cable out approximately eighteen (18) inches from the wall, then fold it back into the wall and tape it onto the thermostat cabling. The thermostat cabling is typically installed by the electrician and should remain outside the scope of work. The same color cable should be used for all cat5e cable for the thermostats. Currently we recommend green. All the green cables should be bundled together, and run into the equipment closet. Leave a space approximately 24" (height) by 18" (width) to mount the thermostat distribution panel. In addition, run a grey cat5e cable for the control from that distribution panel to the equipment rack. That will tie the HVAC distribution panel to the overall integrated control system.

Keep the Communication Going

When the cabling is finished, there's little else on the job that you'll do in terms of HVAC installation. However, there's a fair amount of coordinating work with the HVAC contractor.

We have included a detailed memorandum to send to the HVAC contractor, and we highly recommend that you copy the builder and the homeowner. Email is the most effective method to send a memo to everyone involved. In our chapter "Opening the Project", we discuss collecting email addresses from everyone on site. This/her makes it easy to create an email distribution list. You can send written documents to groups of people at the same time. Email accomplishes two things: it assures you everyone has been informed, and it provides you with a record of your communications with the owner and the other contractors. This/her can help resolve potential miscommunication problems.

Unfortunately, it is not enough to send a memo to the HVAC contractor. You also must call him/her to make sure that he/she understands it, and you have to follow up with him/her during the project.

More often than not you will run into an HVAC contractor, who does not want to install the communicating thermostats. We recommend you go directly to your local rep for Aprilaire, as they will be very helpful in convincing the HVAC contractor to install the thermostats needed for the integrated system. They also will provide the training needed for HVAC installer. To enlist Aprilaire's help, all you have to do is call and ask for a residential specific person. (Note: We have provided complete contact information in the appendix) Provide the name and contact information for the HVAC contractor. Give the representative a copy of the memorandum you sent to the HVAC contractor, and turn that whole process over to the representative. Now you've got someone to give the HVAC contractor technical support; someone who can talk and understand HVAC systems. And you are free from that process.

Termination

Your termination team will install the distribution panel, and terminate all of the cables per Aprilaire's installation directions. We have provided termination instructions in the installation section of the chapter, as well as included all appropriate documentation on the download. In addition terminate the grey cat5e cable that connects the distribution panel to the integrated system equipment rack. Remember to **LABEL ALL CABLES** upon passing cable test.

System Programming

Another step is programming of the system. In the customer information section for this/her chapter are several tables for the customer to fill out his/her preferences. Keypads to operate and control the thermostats should be programmed before you bring them to the home. Then you will not have to program anything in your customer's home, and all that will be left is the final connections.

You simply connect the cables behind the thermostat, and flip the power switch. It should take no more than one person one day to complete the project.

Electronics

The next step is at the end of the job. You need to make sure that the HVAC system is working fully. We have included two memoranda to the customer. One goes out at the beginning of the project, and the other goes out at the end of the project. Within that second memo we explain that the HVAC system must be fully functional for thirty (30) days prior to activating the integration system. This/her is done to cover your own ass. In other words, it would be very easy for the HVAC contractor to blame his/her problems on your system, and ultimately on you rather than accept the responsibility. But if the HVAC contractor can provide a heating system that is fully functional for thirty (30) days, one that is balanced and tweaked and problem free for thirty (30) days, it should be pretty straight forward to connect the HVAC system to the integration system. And if there is a problem, it will be easier to determine in which system the problem lies.

Training

The last step is training the customer to use the keypads for the integration system. We discuss training in the chapter, "Keypads and Touchscreens." We discuss what information should be included on the touchscreen for the HVAC system to make it very simple to use.

The "HVAC Contractor" Letter

Dear Sirs:

(Customer Name), who is building a home on the site of the above address, has hired (Company Name) to install a digital integration system in (Customer Last Name) home. The project will include connecting your HVAC system to our integration system.

My name is (PM Name), and I will be the project manager for the integration project. I will be your contact person for our company throughout the project.

(Company Name) designs, sells and installs custom electronic integration systems that provide entertainment, convenience and comfort in today's digital home. The integration system also enhances security in the home, and provides additional convenience for the customer.

To comply with (Customer Name) decision to hire us to install a home integration system, we request your assistance. The HVAC system will be part of the integrated system. Therefore, we will need you to install Aprilaire 8870 communicating thermostats when you install your HVAC system. On behalf of your customer, we ask that you purchase these thermostats directly from Aprilaire, and install them with the rest of your system. After you have finished your installation, and you are satisfied the HVAC system is working properly, we will provide and install the communications panels and tie communication connections from

NOTES

Send this/her letter at the start of the project, copying the builder, architect, and customer.

Follow up immediately with a telephone call to ensure the HVAC contractor has not only received it but understands his/her responsibilities.

You should determine if the contractor is going to require technical assistance. If required connect him with he local Aprilaire sales representative, who will understand the complex HVAC issues and how to integrate these thermostats with the system.

221

the thermostats to our system. We will provide a quick disconnect from your system.

Cabling Requirements

The thermostats are electronic, and therefore, you should allow sufficient cabling to provide 24Vac to the thermostat. Aprilaire recommends using a standard eight-conductor thermostat cable. After you or the electricians cable the thermostats, we will tape a green category-5e cable to the original thermostat cable. The Cat5e cable will allow communication between the integrated system and the thermostat. Please leave our cable taped to the thermostat cable to enable us to access it when we are ready.

The HVAC System Design

The Aprilaire thermostat works like any other thermostat. The overall design of your system can remain exactly the same. Simply design and install your system as you would if there were no integrated system. The only difference will be substituting the Aprilaire 8870 thermostats for whatever thermostats you normally install.

We have available copies of the thermostat installation manual to help guide you through the design process. In addition, you may call Aprilaire technical support at (800) 782-8638 or visit them at **www.aprilaire.com**.

Radiant Heat Zones

Since radiant heat zones are designed to be left without change during the heating period, we strongly recommend against using Aprilaire communicating 8870 thermostats for these zones, and also recommend against integrating them.

Purchasing the Thermostats

You can purchase the 8870 thermostats directly from local HVAC distributors. It takes about one to two weeks to receive the Aprilaire thermostat. You can find these distributors at **www. aprilaire.com.**

Non–Standard HVAC Systems

Some systems are designed to use non–standard thermostats. If the system being installed cannot accept standard thermostats then we request that you provide a dry contact closure in your system for each of the following setbacks: "Home", "Away", "Vacation", and "Night". That means a total of four contact closure inputs are must be installed for our system. It is outside the scope of our work to determine which thermostats or what setback points are programmed for each of these setbacks.

Your assistance is very much appreciated. If you have any questions, please call me. I will make every effort to provide whatever information you may need.

Sincerely yours,

(PM Name)

(Title and Contact Information)

NOTES

N O T E S

9

SECURITY INTEGRATION

What's Inside

Simple to Complex Integration

Zeroing in on Zones

Working with your Security Contractor

Proposing Security Integration

Chapter Nine

What is a Security System?

A common mistake people make when trying to design something completely foolproof is to underestimate the ingenuity of complete fools.

– Douglas Noel Adams (1952–) English humorist and science fiction novelist

A security system creates and maintains a safe environment. Making a home secure is another major component of an integrated system. There are a number of key elements in a quality security system that make it one that provides the security your customer wants and needs to protect his/her property and family. Chances are that you are not a licensed security contractor, and that's just fine. Providing a security system is a profession all its own. We will discuss in general what a security system provides for the customer, and then will go into describing how best to integrate with the system.

The Master Control Panel

The Master Control Panel is the boss of the outfit. It controls the detection, communication and annunciation (some security systems will talk to you, i.e. bedroom window open) capabilities of the security system. In order to be effective, the master control panel must have a battery backup in case of power failures that ultimately will occur during bad weather or other electrical malfunctions in the community.

The master control panel also has a digital keypad that your customer will use to turn on and off the alarm system. The keypad also is used for administering the system. When your customer or other authorized person arms or disarms the system, it will delay briefly activating the process to allow them time to enter or exit the home. Keep in mind that this feature also can compromise security because the master control panel usually is installed near an entrance, which could be used in a break–in.

228

Sensing Devices

Sensing devices are connected to the master control panel by protective loops or zones. The signals occur between the sensors and the master control panel using hard–wired circuits or radio wave transmission. Many types of sensors are available. The most effective alarm systems use a combination of the following devices:

Motion Detectors, which sense movement using many different technologies. These include: passive infrared, ultrasonic, micro-wave, infrared beam (continuous and visible), or "dual technology" detectors that combine more than one type of detector. Dual technology detectors are the most efficient method in sensing movement.

Magnetic Contacts, which are used on doors and windows. They send a signal to the control panel which interprets it when contact is broken.

Audio Glass Break Detectors, which can be designed to send a signal to the master control panel only when a low–pitched thump from a blow to the glass is followed by a high–pitched crash of breaking glass.

Vibration Detectors, which are closely related to the glass break detectors. They can be adjusted to sense abnormal vibrations in a particular zone in the home.

Foil tape, which usually is applied to the interior surfaces of glass windows or doors. If the glass breaks, the circuit is opened and an alarm signal is sent to the control panel, which it interprets. Generally this type of motion sensor is used on basement windows.

Communication Modules, which usually consist of digital technology connected to a Central Station alarm service. The service monitors the signals of many customers. Basically, the primary connection is through phone lines, which can be easily located and cut. In newer large homes, telephone cable generally is run through a conduit that is buried and run into the house at a hidden location. However, to help alleviate the issues with this potential problem, most of today's systems incorporate the following:

- A line seizing device (such as a RJ–31X jack), which seizes an available phone line in an alarm situation even if the line is busy or if a burglar has jammed the line on purpose,

- A phone line continuity protection device, which can send an alarm signal even if the phone line circuit has been interrupted, and

- A backup communication, which provides a link to the Central Station. This is accomplished either by using a cellular telephone, or a two–way radio transmitter, which is preferable. There also are one–way transmitters on the market, but they do not allow back and forth communication needed to maintain line supervision.

Other security adjuncts or implements also are available today. These include: local alarms, sirens, horns, bells, floodlights, and more. These devices activate at the home in response to a signal from one or more of the sensing devices. They can be effective in scaring off the non–professional thief. However, it is doubtful that they would be effective against a professional thief.

Video Surveillance

Closed Curcuit Television (CCTV) video surveillance systems can either passively record and play back video at certain intervals, be actively monitored by security personnel, or use a combination of these methods.

Generally, CCTV video surveillance is successful in reducing and preventing crimes and is helpful in prosecuting individuals caught in the act of committing a crime.

CCTV surveillance began in banks in the early 1960s, and later in commercial buildings. By the 1970s, CCTV surveillance was also used in hospitals, all–night convenience stores, art galleries, and in many other commercial locations. Video technology improved during the mid–1980s with the introduction of camcorder technology, and in the 1990s with digital and multiplexer technology.

Video cameras now have powerful zoom lenses which can tilt and pan to offer 360–degree coverage. They also are able to gather sharp, clear images in extremely low light. Moreover, new digital video technology requires less labor intensive monitoring. Digital video surveillance cameras can link computer data processing power with sensor or motion detectors to filter out unrelated activities. Such systems can search through a video database of events, allowing the user to isolate only those details in which a particular image occurs.

Many businesses use CCTV surveillance technology to protect products and to promote safe workplace and consumer environments. This trend is now extending to private residences that are placing digital video surveillance cameras both inside and outside the home.

While the security system contractor will provide and install the CCTV surveillance equipment, we as integrators should provide the video cameras on unused television channels in the home. This will give the customer the ability to view these cameras on the television they already own, without the need for special CCTV monitors. In addition we should provide these cameras on video enable touchscreen. We have included more on this topic in the "Keypads & Touchscreens" chapter.

Security System Summary

Employing a security system in the modern home requires a dedicated professional to ensure the home is safe from fire, invasion, and other critical issues, such as flooding, carbon monoxide, and freezing. It is your role as the home integrator to use that information to extend the capabilities of the other systems in the home. This includes interacting with lighting, HVAC, and entertainment systems in the home based on events that happen within the security system. The customer proposal lays out what specificly your company will provide the customer.

Customer Proposal

NOTES

Offering integration with the security system only makes sense when you have included lighting and HVAC integration. The integration interacts with these systems as well as the entertainment system.

Offer the Basic Security Integration to most customers, as it provides most with more than enough automation.

The Basic Security Integration is a great start in understanding how the integration of the

The Advanced Security Integration will require at least one touchscreen for customer settings. The basic does not.

Security is a concern of most homeowners today. You want to protect your property, and most of all your family. There are simple ways to provide some security for your home, such as motion detectors and flood lights; and also more effective, complex ways, such as digitally–controlled security systems. While we are do not offer security systems, we do offer integration for both basic and advanced digitally–controlled security systems. We will work with your security contractor to provide a seamless fit between the security system and the overall integrated system.

Basic Security Integration

A basic integrated security system activates "Home" and "Away" scenes with the activation of your alarm system. When you enter your home and deactivate the security system, the lighting, music, and thermostats will adjust to your preferred home settings. In addition the lights will be programmed to turn on in the event of a fire, panic alarm or break–in. Any security system on the market can be used in basic integration.

Advanced Security Integration

When your security contractor has installed a Napco Gemini 9600 panel, we will integrate it with the other systems in your home. Each of the following features can be enabled or disabled from the setup page on your **touchscreen.**

● "Home" and "Away" mode triggered upon activation and deactivation of the security system.

● Upon burglar or fire event the lighting system will activate the appropriate lighting scenes.

● Upon entrance to the home, via opening a door, lighting will be activated after sunset.

● Upon activation of motion sensors in the home, lighting will be activated after sunset.

Security Camera Integration

When your security contractor provides and installs cameras, we will then provide the ability to view the cameras on every TV in your home. In order to provide this feature we will filter the incoming cable TV signal to provide in–house channels starting at channel 86. This will remove any of the digital cable information from the in–house cable. While we can still provide digital cable to any location that has a surround sound wallplate, other locations will consist of basic cable and the in–house channels. In addition digital cable boxes will be unable to view the in–house channels, and any location that has a digital–cable box, will also require a VCR for reception of the in–house channels.

Customer Information

Below is a list of features available with "Advanced Security Integration". While you will have the ability to enable and disable these features from the setup page of your touchscreen, we initialize your system with you preferences.

Figure 9.1
Security
Integration
Options

Do you want the house to enter the "Home" mode when the alarm is disarmed?	Yes
Do you want the house to enter the "Away" mode when the alarm is armed?	Yes
Do want a "Floor On" scene to come on when the house is disarmed if after dusk?	No
Do you want motion sensors to turn on lighting scenes if in the night mode?	No

NOTES

The options shown to the right are required for the "Advanced Alarm Integration". It is required as part of the progamming phase.

During the proposal stage you specify the quantity of cameras. During the programming phase collect the camera locations from the security contractor. Then confirm in writing with the customers.

Below is a list of camera locations in your home and the assigned in-house channel. Note: These cameras are to be installed and provided by others. Each camera should have a video signal supply to the TV distribution panel in the electronics closet. We have contacted your security provider to communicate these needs.

Figure 9.2
Camera
Locations

Camera Location	Channel
Front Door	86
Side Door	88
Garage & Driveway	90

The "Basic Security Integration" Letter

Dear Sirs:

(Customer Name), who is building a home on the site of the above address, has hired (Company Name) to install a digital integration system in (Customer Last Name) home. The project will include connecting your security system to our integration system.

My name is (PM Name), and I will be the project manager for the integration project. I will be your contact person for our company throughout the project.

(Company Name) designs, sells and installs custom electronic integration systems that provide entertainment, convenience and comfort in today's digital home. The integration system also enhances security in the home, and provides additional convenience for the customer.

We request that you install two relay outputs from your security system. Please provide these relays to a USOC RJ11 Telephone jack next to your panel. This will provide a quick disconnect from the integration system to this telephone jack.

The relays will be used as follows:

- **Armed Status** – The first relay is to output a closure when the system is armed. Please cable it to Pins 3, 6 on the telephone

NOTES

This letter is to be sent to the security contractor during the project open phase. Follow the letter with a telephone call to ensure the security contractor understands his/her responsibilities to the customer.

Copy the architect, builder, and customer on this and another letter that goes to the security contractor.

During the programming phase of the project contact the security contractor once again to ensure that he/she has been able to meet the needs of the customer. If required resend the letter to all parties.

235

jack.

- **Alarm Event**– The second relay is to output a closure when the system goes into alarm mode. Please cable it to Pins 4, 5 the telephone jack.

Your assistance in meeting the customer's request is very much appreciated. If you have any questions, please call me. I will make every effort to provide whatever information you may need.

Sincerely yours,

(PM Name)

(Title and Contact Information)

The "Advanced Security Integration" Letter

NOTES

This letter is to be sent to the security contractor during the project open phase. Follow the letter with a telephone call to insure the security contractor understands his/her responsibilities to the customer.

Copy the architect, builder, and customer on this an another letter that goes to the security contractor.

During the programming phase of the project contact the security contractor once again to insure that he/she has been able to meet the needs of the customer. If required resend the letter to all parties.

Dear Sirs:

(Customer Name), who is building a home on the site of the above address, has hired (Company Name) to install a digital integration system in (Customer Last Name) home. The project will include connecting your security system to our integration system.

My name is (PM Name), and I am project manager for the integration project. I will be your contact person for our company throughout the project.

(Company Name) designs, sells and installs custom electronic integration systems that provide entertainment, convenience and comfort in today's digital home. The integration system also enhances security in the home, and provides additional convenience for the customer.

To comply with (Customer Name) decision to hire us to install a home integration system, we request your assistance. When you install the alarm system, you will need to use a Napco Gemini Panel. Each of these products is compatible with our integrated system. You will need to purchase an RS–232 panel directly from either Napco.

Please review the information below and fax me this sheet with the requested zone numbers filled in. We need this information to program our

237

system appropriately.

A list of "Events" that enhance the home's security is listed below, along with certain installation instructions.

The Siren Event

Please install a relay on the siren signal and connect it to a zone input on the panel. Cable the siren output relay trigger to the last zone number on the system. This zone is programmed as a bypass, auxiliary zone, and is silent with no communication. Enter this zone number below.

Siren Zone Number: _____

We will program lights in the home to respond in the following way.

• On Zone Open: If it is nighttime, all exterior lights will turn on, and the post lights will blink.

• On Zone Open Restore: The post lights will stop blinking, and stay on. The lights will not go off when the siren stops.   All exterior lights must be turned off manually. In addition, the lighting is programmed to turn off all exterior lights in the morning at sunrise.

The Fire Event

Please fill in all fires zones listed below.
Fire Zone Numbers: _____

We will program the lights in the home to respond in the hollowing way.

• On Zone Open: If it is nighttime, all exterior lights will turn on, and the post lights will blink.

• On Zone Open Restore: The post lights stop blinking, and stay on. The lights will not go off when the siren stops.   All exterior lights must be turned off manually. In addition, the lighting is programmed to turn off all exterior lights in the morning at sunrise.

Armed Status Partition 1 to Away Event

Triggered automatically when the customer arms his/her system. It assumes that all zones in the home are programmed into partition one. We will program the system so that the home responds in the following way.

- The music system will turn off. Common area lights will fade to off over a 30–second period, bedrooms are not included. Thermostats are set to a pre–determined "Away" mode. If it is nighttime, exterior lights will turn on.

Armed Status Partition 1 to Home Event

Triggered automatically when the customer arms his/her system

to night home mode (going to bed for the night). It assumes that all zones in the home are programmed into partition 1.

We will program the home to respond in the following way.

- Music system will turn off. Common area lights will fade to off over a 30–second period, bedrooms not included. Thermostats switch to a pre–determined "Night" mode. If it is nighttime, exterior lights will turn on. The "Night" Mode lighting is turned on. This will allows motions to turn on lights in pathways to a low level when triggered.

System Disarm Event

Triggered when the customer disarms his/her system.

We will program the home to respond in the following way.

- Music system set to pre–determined "Home" mode. Thermostats set to pre–determined "Home" mode. Lighting set to pre–

determined "Home" mode.

Door Event

Lights will turn on when someone enters the home. Please fill in all door zones listed below.

Zone Number	Zone Name

We will program the home to respond in the following way.

• On Zone Open: If alarm system is armed, the light inside doorway will turn on. The lights will not go off. All lights must be turned off manually.

Motion Event

Lights turn on when someone enters a given area of the home. Please fill in all motion zones listed below.

Zone Number	Zone Name

We will program the home to respond in the following way.

- On Zone Open: If the home is in "Night" mode, the system will turn on lights to a low level.
- On Zone Open Restore: A timer will set and turn off lights after 15 minutes.

Your assistance in filling out the zone numbers is very much appreciated. If you have any questions, please call me. I will make every effort to provide whatever information you may need.

Sincerely yours,

(PM Name)

(Title and Contact Information)

Steps to Security Integration

Since the security contractor will be installing the actual alarm system, the amount of work required is limited to working with the alarm contractor. The only installation work that needs to be done, is the category 5e cable should be run from the alarm panel to the equipment rack, terminating both sides with T568B standard.

For working with the alarm contractor, we've generated two letters. There are two types of alarm integration – basic and advanced. You can generate the appropriate letter for each system. You'll find that if the alarm contractor hasn't worked with you before, you're better off sticking with the basic integration. It's difficult to find an alarm contractor who is willing or capable of installing an advanced integration system. But something that you can work towards with the alarm contractor.

Project Open

Send out the letter to the alarm contractor. And through the project, up until the customer moves into his/her home, it's your job as project manager to keep in close contact with the alarm contractor to assure that he/she knows his/her responsibilities.

Cabling

Run a grey cat5e from the integrated control system equipment rack location to the security panel location, utilizing a cabling sticker to annotate the security panel's location.

Termination

Install a male RJ45 at each end of the grey cat5e control terminated to T568B standard **(see figure 9.4)**. Leave enough length at

242

each end to plug into each system. Test and label!

System Programming

The information from the alarm contractor is going to be required during the customer preference gathering phase, which happens before you put in the finish electronics. That phase is covered in more detail in the chapter, "Keypads and Touchscreens."

Electronics

After the system is fully installed and functional you can then patch in the cat5e cable you have run and terminated to the control system. Attach a set of DB9 to RJ45 connectors to the end of the grey cat5e control cable and connect to the security and control system.

Training

Help your customer understand how the system works, by reviewing in person each of the customer perferences. Ensure each video camera is visible on the designated channel. Remember training not only extends to your customer but the security contractor.

NOTES

NOTES

10

THEATER
INTEGRATION

What's Inside

A Brief Look at Home Theater

Chapter Ten

Introduction

This chapter is intentionally left small, as the home theater subject will be covered in greater detail in a separate book.

The Home Theater Proposal

Your customer will more than likely want to know the total cost of all the systems that will be designed for and installed in his/her home. We recommend that you prepare two separate proposals, one for the home integration system, and the second for the home theater and all audio/video systems. The audio/video systems include: surround receiver, DVD player, VCR, television, and CD player. By keeping the home theater and audio/video systems out of the main home integration proposal, you can delay choosing all the consumer electronics until the construction of the home is completed. This will allow you to focus your attention on the integration infrastructure for the music, lighting, HVAC, and security systems during the home construction. There will be plenty of work involved with the design and implementation of these systems.

We also recommend that you prepackage the audio/video systems to present to your customer. This idea is similar to the installation kits recommended in an earlier chapter. The advantage of prepackaging is that it simplifies your customer's choices and it provides a better pricing strategy.

During the proposal phase, emphasize to your customer how critical the decisions are for the main home integration system. Explain how important it is to design and install an integration infrastructure that is flexible, and that this flexibility will allow decisions about the audio/video systems to be made later. Also explain that this flexibility in the infrastructure will allow your customer to make design choices for the home theater system later in the process.

Separate But Connected

Each of the audio/video systems can be designed to work as a stand-alone system. However, each system also can be connected to the main integrated system. Remember our golden rule "Design with Backups". You want your customer to be able to retain functionality for most of the system, if there is a failure elsewhere in the system.

Generally, the main integrated control system is installed in the equipment rack in the basement. Its purpose is to control the lighting, HVAC, security, and music systems. If you choose to take the infrared (IR) and RS232 output from the centralized control and send these signals to the remote audio/video system, you can wind up with mega problems. Here's why.

Sending IR and RS232 commands over long distances (those greater than 25 feet) are unreliable. Interference from other cables in the home can degrade these signals, making them insufficient and ineffective. Even if you can get the signals working today, that is no guarantee they will work tomorrow.

A failure in the main system will cause a failure in the local system. In the event that there is a failure somewhere in the main system (eventually all things fail) there should be as little impact on your customer's home as possible. By designing each system to be a standalone system, you will prevent a failure from spreading throughout the home.

Here is an example.

The family room surround system has a separate controller that controls the local surround receiver, DVD player, VCR, television, and CD player. In addition the wireless touchscreen in the room allows selection and control of the home-wide music server. This is the music server we discussed in the "Music Integration" chapter, and is connected to the home-wide music system.

In order to listen to that source, a zone on the music system is connected via the music output wallplate to the AUX input on the receiver. In order to control the server the local controller talks with the centralized control, which in turn tells the music system to select the music server. So now let's assume there is a failure in the home–wide music system. This will prevent any of the speakers in the home from functioning properly. However, the customer will still be able to watch DVDs, video tapes, and television without interruption. Certainly they can no longer listen to the music server in the home, but they have not lost complete functionality of every system in the home.

Creating a Shell

The following is a brief discussion of three types of audio/video systems for which you can provide a shell for your customer during the construction process.

The Master Bedroom Audio/Video System

A typical master bedroom is shown in figure 10.1. It this scenario we have a customer who would like to have the plasma television installed over the fireplace on the wall across from the bed. The other request is that the room work like every other room in the home, so the customer can listen to music, control lights, and adjust the thermostats. The required cables to accommodate these options are listed below.

RG6QD–BK – This cable provides cable television to the VCR or cable box.

RG6QD–WH – This cable provides satellite reception to the satellite receiver. Devices such as Tivo require two connections for satellite, so your customer may record and view at the same time. If this is the case, then the RG6QD–BK cable can be used by adding a diplexer to both ends. A diplexer adds and removes satellite reception to a coaxial cable with a cable TV signal on it.

16/2 – These speaker cables are connected to the in–wall speakers located on the left and right of the television.

14/4 – This speaker cable attaches to the 16/2 speaker cables straight through to the speakers in the room. In the electronics room equipment rack this cable is connected to the music system amplifier. The master bedroom is set up as a zone on the music system.

Cat5e–PK – Two of these cables are included with the wallplate. The first is used to connect to the unbalanced–to–balanced wallplate device. This will send full–volume music from the audio output of the local equipment to the centralized music system. A set of interconnects then connect the wallplate to the output of an audio/video switch located in the master bedroom equipment rack. The second cable can be used to double up the conductors for runs longer than

300 feet. It also can be used to attach video conversion baluns to send composite video to/from the centralized system.

Cat5e–BL – This cable provides an in-home networking connection for Internet protocol–(IP–) based devices. Devices, such as Tivo and some surround receivers, now have IP–based connects to access information from the Internet.

Cat5e–WH – This cable is used to provide a plain old telephone to devices such as satellite receivers.

18/2pr–BL – This cable is used to connect the wireless touch-screen's radio frequency (RF) receiver located in the closet with the centralized integrated control system.

Cat5e–GY – This cable is used to connect the control system located in the room with the centralized integrated control system.

Equipment Rack
Location

Wireless
Touchscreen

Dressing Closet

Multimedia &
Music Input
Wallplates

16/2 WH

Plasma TV
Mounted over
fireplace

2" ID Conduit
Video and control cables are run through the conduit

14/4 BL spliced to 16/2 WH
18/2pr BL for touchscreen
(2) cat5ePK for music wallplate
RG6BK, RG6WH, cat5eWH, cat5eBL
for multimedia wallplate.

16/2 WH

To
Electronics
Closet in
Basement

Master Bedroom

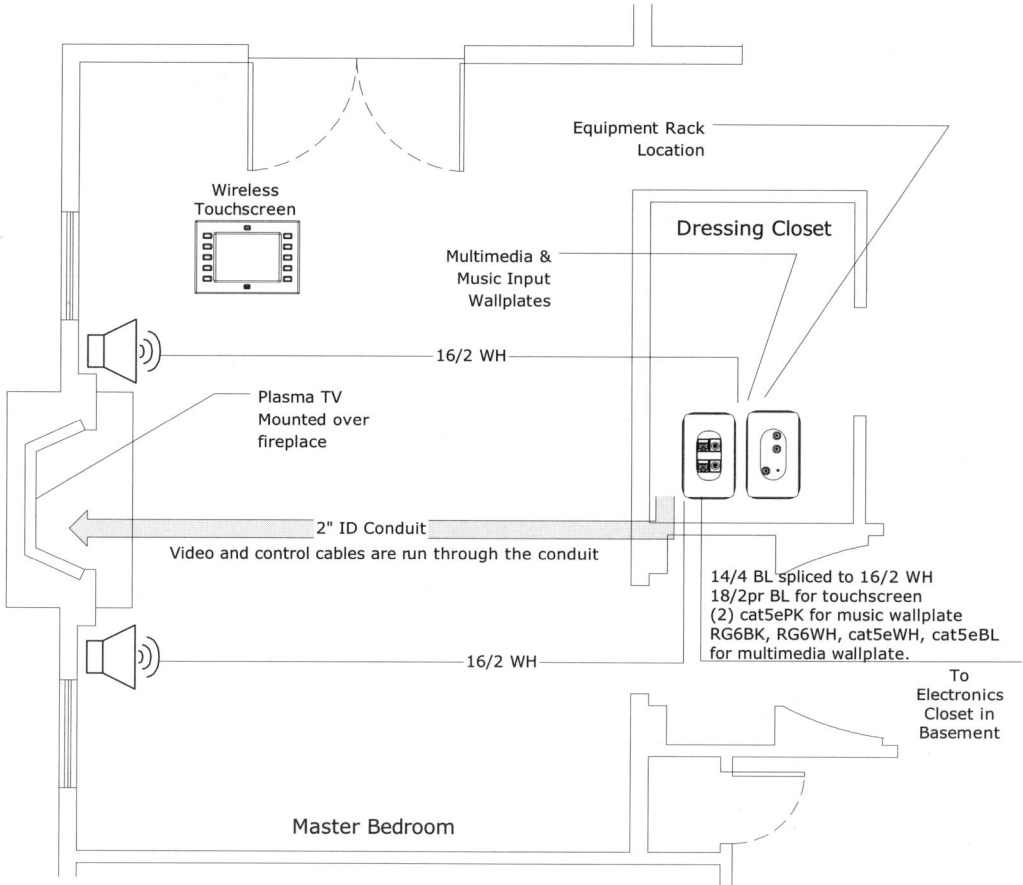

Figure 10.1
Master Bedroom
Audio/Video System

The Family Room Surround Sound System

The cables for the surround sound theater system are listed below. It is important to design the theater as a shell at the start of the home construction. Allow for as much flexibility in its design to give you and your customer the freedom to make choices when time is not as critical as it is during the building process. A sample family room theater system is shown in Figure 10.2.

RG6QD–BK – The wallplate includes two of these cables so the customer may record and play cable programs simultaneously. These cables provide the cable programming signal to the VCR, cable box, and the television.

RG6QD–WH – The wallplate includes two of these cables, which provide satellite reception to the satellite receiver. Devices, such as Tivo, require two connections for satellite to enable your customer to record and view at the same time.

16/2 – These speaker cables are connected to the surround speakers. On the wallplate side they provide a connection for the receiver's surround speaker output.

14/4 – This cable is used when the room is set up in theater mode. It is used if a home theater is not chosen for the room. You never know what will get deleted or changed during the construction process. If the customer asks, you can attach the 14/4 speaker cables straight through to the speakers in the room. Thus changing the surround speakers into music speakers.

Cat5e–PK – The wallplate includes two of these cables. The first is used to connect to the unbalanced–to–balanced wallplate device. This will send full-volume music from the centralized music system to the wallplate. A set of interconnects then connect the wallplate to the AUX input of the surround sound receiver. The second cable can be used to double up the conductors for runs longer than 300 feet.

The cable also can be used to attach video conversion baluns to send composite video to/from the centralized system. It can also be used to connect a second unbalanced–to–balanced wallplate to connect a local six–disc CD player, which will play through the central music system.

Cat5e–BL – This cable provides an in–home networking connection for IP–based devices. Devices, such as Tivo and some surround receivers, now have IP–based connects to access information from the Internet.

Cat5e–WH – This cable is used to provide plain old telephone to devices, such as satellite receivers.

Cat5e–GY – This cable is used to connect the local control system for the audio/video device that is located in the family room with the centralized integrated control system.

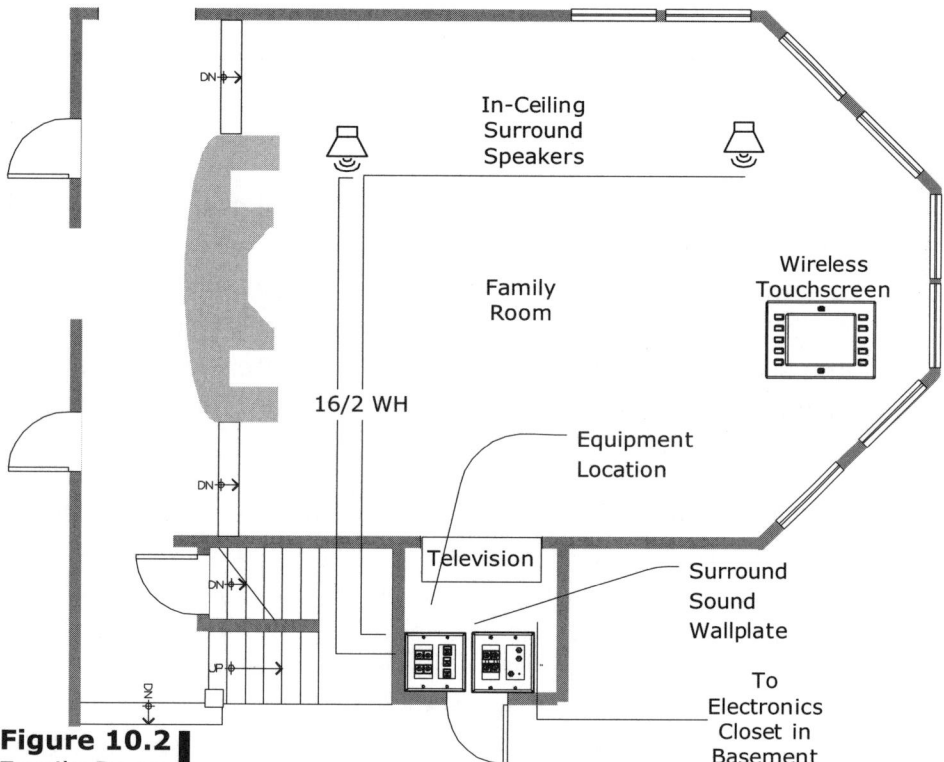

Figure 10.2
Family Room
Surround Sound

The Dedicated Home Theater

This theater is typically located in a basement or in a bonus area above the garage. The space is dedicated to the purpose of watching movies, sports, and video games. The lighting is controlled through both lamps in the room and windows, which are covered with light–blocking shades or are not present at all.

To prepare for this theater, install a surround sound wallplate in a dedicated electronics closet attached to the theater room. We recommend installing the DVD player, VCR, and surround processor in a cabinet that faces inside the theater, or its lobby. The back of the cabinet is in the theater's electronics closet. Then install two–inch O.D. (outside dimension) conduit as shown in figure 10.3.

We recommend providing a shell for the theater because it takes the pressure off of you and your customer to make theater and audio/video decisions too quickly. It allows you to focus on the integrated system and its design. Once the project is well underway and time permits, you can start to focus on the design of the theater with your customer.

The surround sound wallplate provides all of the same connections as laid out in the family room theater. However, there is one small change. You don't install the speaker cables, which are the 16/2–WH to the surround speakers. Instead you install a conduit system so the speaker cables may be installed at a later time. In addition you don't install the 14/4–BL speaker cable from the music system to the theater.

Installing flexible two–inch O.D. conduit allows you to provide name brand cables as part of the theater system. Since these cables are premium in their nature, it is far safer to add them after all of the home construction is finished. This will avoid the possibility of inadvertent damage to the cables, thus sacrificing performance. The other major reason for the conduit is to allow for future upgrades and changes. Theater technology changes rapidly. For example, over the past few years in looking at the video feed to the projector it has changed from s–video to component video to RGB to DVI. So what connections might your projector require for top performance? How will the subwoofers be cabled? What connections are required for the screen? All of these questions can be answered with the most current technology because conduit has been installed for the theater.

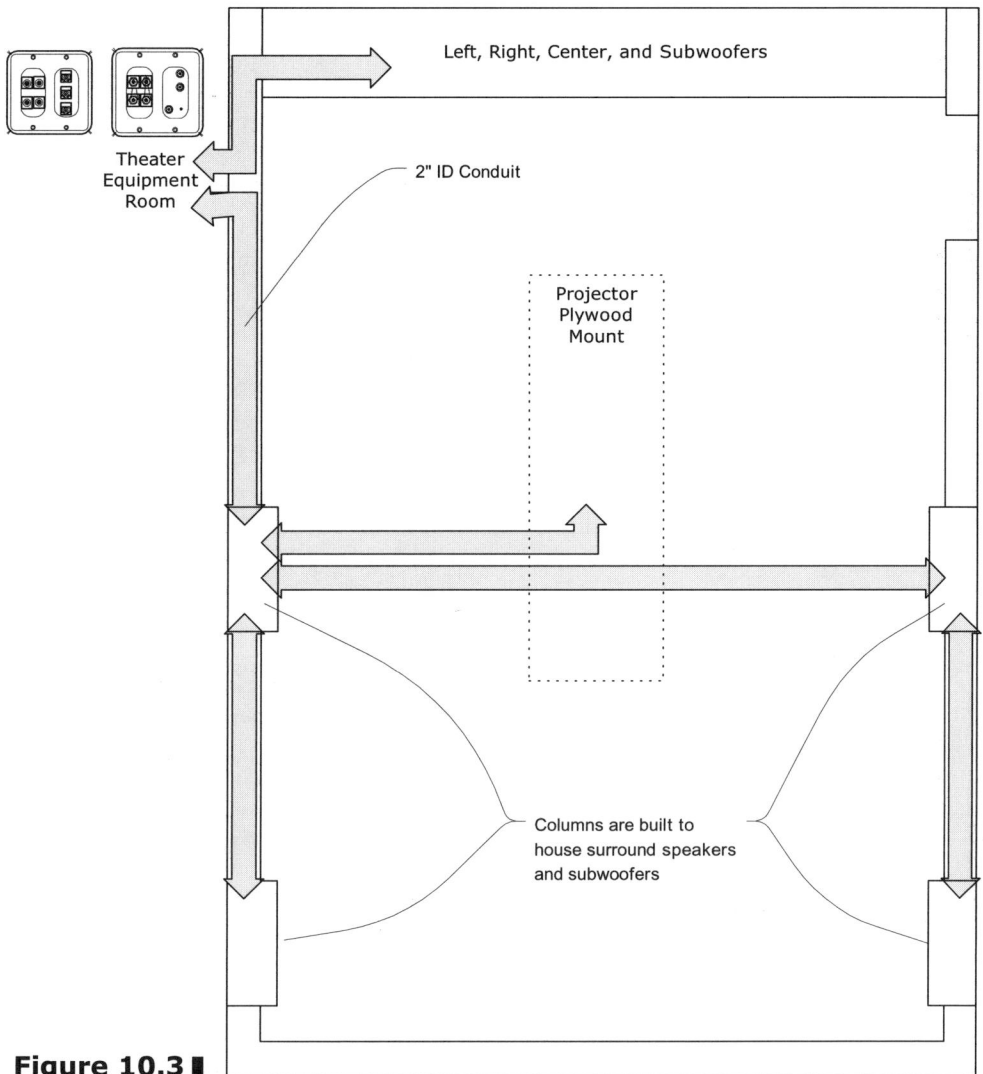

Left, Right, Center, and Subwoofers

Theater
Equipment
Room

2" ID Conduit

Projector
Plywood
Mount

Columns are built to
house surround speakers
and subwoofers

Figure 10.3
Dedicated Theater
System

N O T E S

NOTES

GLOSSARY OF TERMS

Glossary of Terms

The following represents the hard work of the home networking council of CEDIA, and have been reprinted with their permission. For more information concerning CEDIA go to **www.cedia.net**.

AAC – (Advanced Audio Coder)

ADSL – A newly standardized transmission technology, facilitating simultaneous use of normal telephone services, data transmission of 6 Mbit/s in the downstream and Basic–Rate Access (BRA).

ADSL Forum – Formed in late 1994 to help telephone companies and their suppliers realize the enormous market potential of ADSL. Assistance comes in two forms – technical and marketing. The Forum's marketing programs attempt to simplify ADSL's inherent technical complexity and spread the news. The Forum's public output therefore mixes the tutorial with the promotional.

Alarm Systems – An assembly of equipment and devices designed and arranged to signal the presence of an alarm condition requiring urgent attention such as unauthorized entry, fire, and temperature rise.

AMR – (Automatic Meter Reading) – A process of reading a meter, preparing and conditioning the data, and transmitting the accumulated data from the meter location to a central data accumulation device (usually a computer). The communications device might be a radio, telephone line, PLC, direct cable or any combination thereof.

Amperage – Amount of electrical current transferred from one component to another. This specification is often important when considering the amplifier loudspeaker interface.

ANSI – (American National Standards Institute) – Founded in 1918, ANSI is a voluntary organization composed of over 1,300 members (including all the large computer companies) that creates standards for the computer industry. For example, ANSI C is a version of the C language that has been approved by the ANSI committee. To a large degree, all ANSI C compilers, regardless of which company produces them, should behave similarly. In addition to programming languages, ANSI sets standards for a wide range of technical areas, from electrical specifications to communications protocols.

API – (Application Programming Interface) – A set of routines, protocols, and tools for building software applications. A good API makes it easier to develop a program by providing all the building blocks. A programmer puts the blocks together. Most operating environments, such as MS–Windows, provide an API so that programmers can write applications consistent with the operating environment. Although APIs are designed for programmers, they are ultimately good for users because they guarantee that all programs using a common API will have similar interfaces. This makes it easier for users to learn new programs.

ARP – (Address Resolution Protocol) – A TCP/IP protocol used to convert an IP address into a physical address (called a DLC address), such as an Ethernet address. A host wishing to obtain a physical address broadcasts an ARP request onto the TCP/IP network. The host on the network that has the IP address in the request then replies with its physical hardware address.

Aspect ratio – The ratio of a picture's width to its height. Typical television aspect ratio is 4:3, while wide screen formats provide greater width of the viewing area.

ATSC – (Advanced Television Systems Committee)

ATVEF – (Advanced Television Enhancement Forum)

AutoIP – Allows devices to claim IP addresses in the absence of a DHCP server or similar configuration authority.

Automation – Automatically controlled operation of an apparatus, process, or system by mechanical or electronic devices that take the place of human organs of observation, effort, and decision.

Bandwidth – The data–carrying capacity of a transmission medium, usually measured in hertz (Hz).

BIOS – (Basic Input /Output System) – Built–in software that determines what a computer can do without accessing programs from a disk. On PCs, the BIOS contains all the code required to control the keyboard, display screen, disk drives, serial communications, and a number of miscellaneous functions. The BIOS is typically placed in a ROM chip that comes with the computer (it is often called a ROM BIOS). This ensures that the BIOS will always be available and will not be damaged by disk failures. It also makes it possible for a computer to boot itself. Because RAM is faster than ROM, though, many computer manufacturers design systems so that the BIOS is copied from ROM to RAM each time the computer is booted. This is known as shadowing.

Bipole – Bi-directional loudspeaker with zero degrees of phase difference between its front and rear acoustical output.

Bit – (Binary Digit) – The smallest unit of digital information, represented by 1 (on) or 0 (off).

Bluetooth – Bluetooth refers to a short-range radio technology aimed at simplifying communications among net devices. It aims to simplify data synchronization between net devices and other computers. Products with Bluetooth technology must be qualified and pass interoperability testing by the Bluetooth Special Interest Group prior to release. The Bluetooth 1.0 specification consists of two documents: the Foundation Core, which provides design specifications, and the Foundation Profile, which provides interoperability guidelines. Bluetooth's founding members include Ericsson, IBM, Intel, Nokia and Toshiba.

Broadband Internet – An Internet transmission medium that has a bandwidth (capacity) capable of carrying numerous voice, video, and data channels simultaneously. Each Channel operates on a different frequency. Cable TV is a broadband transmission medium.

Browser – (Web browser) – A software application used to locate and display Web pages. The two most popular browsers are Netscape Navigator and Microsoft Internet Explorer. Both of these are graphical browsers, which means that they can display graphics as well as text. In addition, most modern browsers can present multimedia information, including sound and video, though they require plug-ins for some formats.

Browser Interface – A program that connects the data obtained from the Internet/Intranet to the computer and displays that data to the human operator (user). The browser interface also allows the user to enter and send data and/or commands via his/her computer over the Internet/Intranet.

Bus Report – Listings of problems found with a product.

Byte – A is a unit of eight (8) bits.

CABA – (Continental Automated Buildings Association) – Source for information, education, and networking relating to home and building automation. Its mission is to encourage the development, promotion and adoption of business opportunities in the home and building automation industry. Members include manufacturers, dealers, installers, telecommunications companies, energy utilities, builders, consultants, research organizations, publishers, educational institutions, governments and associations.

Cable Modem – An external device that hooks up to your computer. Instead of getting an Internet connection through your telephone wire (or another system), you get a connection through your cable network (same place your cable TV connection comes from).

CATV– Community Antenna Television

Category 3 – Four (4) twisted pairs of high–capacity wire enclosed in an insulated sheath. Handles telephone signals for phones, faxes and modems, plus video and data signals. Transfers data at 10 Mbits (mega bits) per second.

Category 5 – (CAT 5) – A rating system that refers to the number of twisted pairs of wires in a telephone cable. The more twists, the greater bandwidth and speed and the less interference in the transmission of voice and computer data. Specifying Cat 5, over the more common Cat 3, is an inexpensive upgrade.

CE – (Consumer Electronics)

CEA – (Consumer Electronics Association) – Addresses questions of public policy, standards development, product marketing and training, which no single or small coalition of companies can address on its own. CEA brings together hundreds of high–tech companies to work on such issues.

CEbus – (Consumer Electronic Bus) – An open standard that specifies requirements for communications between and interoperability of products in home or light–commercial environments. It specifies the required communications protocol, network object and product models.

CEDIA – (Custom Electronic Design and Installation Association) – A trade association for designers and installers of high–end audio/video and automation systems.

Channel – (1) In communications, the term channel refers to a communications path between two computers or devices. It can refer to the physical medium (the wires) or to a set of properties that distinguishes one channel from another. For example, TV channels refer to particular frequencies at which radio waves are transmitted. IRC channels refer to specific discussions. (2) For IBM PS/2 computers, a channel is the same as an expansion bus. (3) In sales and marketing, the way in which a vendor communicates with and sells products to consumers.

Center channel loudspeaker – Single loudspeaker, which sits in front or on top of a television screen which reproduces the dialog of a movie in a surround sound system.

CLEC – (Competitive Local Exchange Carrier [pronounced see–lek]) – A telephone company that competes with an Incumbent Local Exchange Carrier (ILEC) such as a Regional Bell Operating Company (RBOC), GTE, ALLNET, etc. With the passage of the Telecommunications Act of 1996, there has been an explosion in the number of CLECs.

Coaxial Cable – Cable used to carry television and FM signals with a characteristic impedance of 75 ohms. It has a center wire, insulation, a tubular conductor (such as conductive pipe, braid, or foil), and more insulation, all centered or "coaxial" about the center wire.

CODEC – encoder/decoder

COFDM– Coded Orthogonal Frequency Division Multiplexing

Compact disc player – Digital source component which reads and converts the binary information from a compact disc into an analog signal which is then fed to the rest of a hi–fi system.

Connectivity – A computer buzzword that refers to the program or device's ability to link with other programs and devices. For example, a program that can import data from a wide variety of other programs and can export data in many different formats is said to have good connectivity. On the other hand, computers that have difficulty linking into a network (many laptop computers, for example) have poor connectivity.

Controlnet – A pathway that carries information and control commands to many devices over a dedicated localized area. For example, from a one IP Internet address.

Control Network – A control network is a group of devices that are networked together to sense, monitor, communicate and control. In some ways, a control network resembles a data network (such as a LAN). Whereas, data networks consist of computers networked together, control networks consist of sensors, actuators and controllers networked together. Similar to data networks, control networks consist of devices attached to various communications media, connected by routers that communicate to one another using a common protocol. Network management software allows administrators to configure and maintain their networks. In control networks the components are optimized for the cost, performance, size and response characteristics of control applications to enable networks to extend into a class of applications that data networking technology cannot reach.

Convergence – (1) The coming together of two or more disparate disciplines or technologies. For example, the so–called fax revolution was produced by a convergence of telecommunications technology, optical scanning technology, and printing technology. (2) In graphics, convergence refers to how sharply an individual color pixel on a monitor appears. Each pixel is composed of three dots – a red, blue, and green one. If the dots are badly misconverged, the pixel will appear blurry. All monitors have some convergence errors, but they differ in degree.

Crestron – A popular total home control product based on a wireless radio–frequency touch panel and central control processor capable of interacting with everything from the thermostat to Nasdaq.

Crossover – Frequency dividing electrical network, which splits an incoming audio signal into ranges best suited to a loudspeaker's various drive elements.

CRT– (Cathode Ray Tube)

DAB – (Digital Audio Broadcasting)

Daisy Chain – A wiring method where each termination point is wired in series from the previous jack. A Daisy Chain is usually not the preferred wiring method, since a break in the wiring would disable all jacks "downstream" from the break.

DARS – (Digital Audio Radio Service)

Data Rate – The maximum number of bits of information that can be transmitted per second, typically expressed as megabytes per second (Mbps).

DBS – (Direct Broadcast Satellite)

Demarcation Point – A point where operational control or ownership changes. Also called the "demarc".

DIY – (Do it Yourself)

DIFM – (Do it For Me)

Differential Amplification – Method of amplifying a signal whereby the output signal is a function of the difference between two input signals.

Digital–to–Analog Converter – Popularly known as a D–A converter, this device accepts an incoming digital bitstream and converts it to an analog electronic signal.

Digital Audio Tape – A digital audio format stored in binary form on a small cassette. Music can be recorded digitally with this format (some restrictions do apply to prevent excessive duplication).

DHCP – (Dynamic Host Configuration Protocol) – A protocol for assigning dynamic IP addresses to devices on a network. With dynamic addressing, a device can have a different IP address every time it connects to the network. In some systems, the device's IP address can even change while it is still connected. DHCP also supports a mix of static and dynamic IP addresses. Dynamic addressing simplifies network administration because the software keeps track of IP addresses rather than requiring an administrator to manage the task. This means that a new computer can be added to a network without the hassle of manually assigning it a unique IP address. Many ISPs use dynamic IP addressing for dial-up users. DHCP client support is built into Windows 95, 98 and NT Workstation. NT 4 Server includes both client and server support.

Digital – Refers to the use of binary code in the storage and transmission of data. In recording audio and video data the images are discrete, non-continuous codes. It provides signal reproduction with little noise or distortion.

Dipole – Bi-directional loudspeaker with 180 degrees of phase difference between its front and rear acoustical output.

Direct view television – Television, which uses a cathode ray tube (CRT) to display a picture.

DLP – (Digital Light Processing (for video projection))

DMCA – (Digital Millennium Copyright Act)

DNS – (Domain Name System (or Service) – An Internet service that translates domain names into IP addresses. Because domain names are alphabetic, they're easier to remember. The Internet however, is really based on IP addresses. Every time you use a domain name, therefore, a DNS service must translate the name into the corresponding IP address. For example, the domain name www.example.com might translate to 198.105.232.4. The DNS system is, in fact, its own network. If one DNS server doesn't know how to translate a particular domain name, it asks another one, and so on, until the correct IP address is returned. A second "DNS" (short for digital nervous system, a term coined by Bill Gates) referrers to a network of personal computers that make it easier to obtain and understand information. In small networks, such as at home or in small business, DNS Servers may not exist.

Dolby AC-3 – Standard from Dolby Laboratories, which incorporates six discrete channels of information for the playback of video soundtracks.

Dolby Pro Logic – Surround sound standard from Dolby Laboratories for the playback of movie soundtracks in the home. The system utilizes five loudspeakers – two main, two rear and a center and a decoder to properly steer the signal to its appropriate channel.

DSL – Refers collectively to all types of (Digital Subscriber Lines), the two main categories being ADSL and SDSL. Two other types of xDSL technologies are High-data-rate DSL (HDSL) and Single-line DSL (SDSL). DSL technologies use sophisticated modulation schemes to pack data onto copper wires. DSL is one of several methods for delivering high-speed, ever-ready access to the Internet, 5 to 30 times as fast as traditional telephone-line modems. It also lets users make and receive phone calls while surfing the net. DSLs are sometimes referred to as last-mile technologies because they are used only for connections from a telephone switching station to a home or office, not between switching stations.

DSS – (Digital Satellite System) – A network of satellites that broadcast digital data. An example of a DSS is DirecTV, which broadcasts digital television signals. DSS's are expected to become more important as the TV and computer converge into a single medium for information and entertainment.

DTCP – (Digital Transmission Content Protection)

DTMF – (Dual Tone Multi-Frequency) – A system used by touch-tone telephones. DTMF assigns a specific frequency, or tone, to each key so that it can easily be identified by a microprocessor.

DTV – (Desktop Video Production) – The production of videos with a personal computer. It is an emerging technology.

DVB – (Digital Video Broadcasting (multi-purpose standard, mostly outside of North America))

DVD – (Digital Versatile Disc or Digital Video Disc) – A new type of CD-ROM that holds a minimum of 4.7GB (gigabytes), enough for a full-length movie. Many experts believe that DVD disks, called DVD-ROMs, will eventually replace CD–ROMs, VHS cassettes and laser discs. The DVD specification supports disks with capacities of from 4.7GB to 17GB and access rates of 600 KBps to 1.3 MBps. One of the best features of DVD drives is that they are backward – compatible with CD–ROMs. This means that DVD players can play old CD–ROMs, CD–I disks, and video CDs, as well as new DVD–ROMs. Newer DVD players, called second–generation or DVD–2 drives, can also read CD–R and CD–RW disks. DVD uses MPEG–2 to compress video data.

DVR – (Digital Video Recorder) – A device that converts the picture into digital signals. These signals can be stored, transferred and searched.

Dynamic loudspeaker – A loudspeaker that uses conventional cone and dome drive elements exclusively.

E–commerce – The process of conducting business on–line. This includes, for example, buying and selling products with digital cash and via Electronic Data Interchange (EDI).

Early Adopter – Beloved by high–tech manufacturers, the early adopter is a consumer willing to try any new technology.

Efficiency – The ratio of a loudspeaker's acoustical output to a given electrical input. A loudspeaker's sound pressure level is measured in decibels.

EIA – (Electronics Industry Alliance)

Electrostatic loudspeaker – Planar loudspeaker, incorporating a charged transducer suspended between two oppositely charged electrodes.

EPAC – (Enhanced Perceptual Audio Codec)

EPG – (Electronic Program Guide)

EPRI – (Electric Power Research Institute) – A non–profit research group dedicated to applied research for its member electric utilities. Its charter includes fundamental and applied research.

Ethernet – A local–area network (LAN) protocol developed by Xerox Corporation in cooperation with DEC and Intel in 1976. Ethernet uses a bus or star topology and supports data transfer rates of 10 Mbps (10Base – T). The Ethernet specification served as the basis for the IEEE 802.3

standard, which specifies the physical and lower software layers. Ethernet uses the CSMA/CD access method to handle simultaneous demands. It is one of the most widely implemented LAN standards. A newer version of Ethernet, called 100Base–T (or Fast Ethernet), supports data transfer rates of 100 Mbps. The newest version, Gigabit Ethernet supports data rates of 1 gigabit (1,000 megabits) per second.

FAQ – (Frequently Asked Questions)

FCC – (Federal Communications Commission)

Frame Relay – A managed shared high–speed circuit.

Frequency Hopping – A communications methodology that transmits over continuously changing random frequency.

Fiber Optics – Plastic or glass cable that carries a large capacity of information using light beams (modulated light waves) and is immune to electrical noise, lightning, and induced voltages. Data, expressed as pulses of light rather than electrons, that are transmitted by lasers or other devices. Fiber–based systems are suited for high volume, and broadband communications. A pair of hair–thin strands can carry the same volume of information as 32,000 pairs of copper communications cables. Fiber is costly and requires sophisticated electronic equipment.

Firewall – A system designed to prevent unauthorized access to or from a private network. Firewalls can be implemented in both hardware and software, or a combination of both. Firewalls are frequently used to prevent unauthorized Internet users from accessing private networks connected to the Internet, especially Intranets. All messages entering or leaving the Intranet pass through the firewall, which examines each message and blocks those that do not meet the specified security criteria.

FireWire – aka: IEEE 1394–1995 – A new, very fast external bus standard that supports data transfer rates of up to 400 Mbps (400 million bits per second). Products supporting the 1394 standard go under different names, depending on the company. Apple, which originally developed the technology, uses the trademarked name FireWire. Other companies use other names, such as I–link and Lynx, to describe their 1394 products. A single 1394 port can be used to connect up 63 external devices. In addition to its high speed, 1394 also supports isochronous data -- delivering data at a guaranteed rate. This makes it ideal for devices that need to transfer high levels of data in real–time, such as video devices. Although extremely fast and flexible, 1394 is also expensive. Like USB, 1394 supports both Plug–and–Play and hot plugging, and also provides power to peripheral devices. The main difference between 1394 and USB is that 1394 supports faster data transfer rates and is more expensive. 1394 is expected to be used mostly for devices that require large throughputs, such as video cameras, whereas USB will be used to connect most other peripheral devices.

Flash Memory – A special type of EEPROM that can be erased and reprogrammed in blocks instead of one byte at a time. Many modern PCs have their BIOS stored on a flash memory chip so that it can easily be updated if necessary. Such a BIOS is sometimes called a flash BIOS. Flash memory is also popular in modems because it enables the modem manufacturer to support new protocols as they become standardized.

Frequency Response – The measurement of an audible signal's amplitude and phase characteristics relative to a given, absolute level.

Front Projection Television – Television which forms an image by projecting a picture from in front of a screen.

FTP – (File Transfer Protocol) – The protocol used on the Internet for sending files.

Gateway – A special node that interfaces two or more dissimilar networks and translates between them (such as between security and lighting controls).

G.Lite – G.Lite is the informal name of what is expected to be the standard way to install ADSL (Asymmetric Digital Subscriber Line) service. Also known as Universal ADSL, G.Lite makes it possible to have Internet connections to home and business computers at up to 1.5 Mbps (millions of bits per second) over regular phone lines. Even at the lowest downstream rate generally offered of 384 Kbps (thousands of bits per second), G.Lite will be about seven times faster than regular phone service with a V.90 modem and three times faster than an ISDN connection. Upstream speeds from the computer will be up to 128 Kbps. (Theoretical speeds for ADSL are much higher, but the data rates given here are what is realistically expected).

GUI – (Graphical User Interface)

HAA – (Home Automation Association) – A trade association for installers and manufacturers of home automation products and systems.

HAPI – (Home Application Programming Interface)

HAVi – (Home Audio/Video Interoperability) – Pertains to interconnecting and controlling AV electronic appliances connected in Home Audio/Video Networks based on IEEE–1394. In May 1998, the HAVi core specification, a core home networks application for AV electronics appliances, was compiled and released by eight companies – GRUNDIG A.G., Hitachi, Ltd., Matsushita Electric Industrial Co., Ltd., Royal Philips Electronics N.V., Sharp Corporation, Sony Corporation, Thomson Multimedia S.A., Toshiba Corporation – The HAVi core specification is being actively promoted as a home network standard for the AV electronics and multimedia industries.

HDCD – An encode/decode process attempting to improve upon the sound quality provided by the original compact disc standard. CD's recorded in HDCD can be played back in a conventional CD player and likewise, a CD player incorporating an HDCD decoder can play back non–HDCD encoded disks.

HDTV – (High Definition Television) – The new digital standard for enhanced picture quality for TV broadcasting that will dramatically increase the number of HRLs (Horizontal Resolution Lines), providing a much sharper picture even if the image is several feet wide. HDTV requires signals that are broadcast in HDTV format.

Home API – The Home API Working Group was founded two years ago to focus on the unique problems of getting PC's and home devices connected and reliably controlled in the home. The Home API Working Group believes that a merge of Home API interests and efforts with the UPnP Forum is in the best interest of Home API developers.

Home Application Server – A program run on a mid–sized machine that handles all application operations between browser–based computers and a company's back–end business applications or databases. Because many databases cannot interpret commands written in HTML, the application server works as a translator, allowing, for example, a customer with a browser to search an online retailer's database for pricing information. Application servers are seen as filling a large and growing market.

Home Automation – The result of installing communicating microprocessor–based products and systems in a home.

Home Network – A home network interconnects electronic products and enables remote access to and control of the products and any available content such as music, video or data.

Home Networking – Home Networking is the technology that allows all electronic devices in the users environment to seamlessly communicate with each other and the outside world.

Home PNA – (Home Phoneline Networking Alliance) – An association of industry–leading companies working together to ensure adoption of a single unified phone line, networking standard and rapidly bring to market a range of interoperable home networking solutions. http://www.HomePNA.org.

Home PnP – (Plug'N Play) – An interoperability specification for consumer products based on the CAL language developed by the CEBus Industry Council usable over any network protocol.

HomeRF Working Group – The mission of the HomeRF Working Group is to enable the existence of a broad range of interoperable consumer devices, by establishing an open industry specification for unlicensed RF digital communications for PCs and consumer devices anywhere, in and around the home.

Home Run – Wiring method that connects each outlet or sensor directly to the electrical, distribution or control panel instead of several outlets/sensors on a continuous loop.

275

Horn loading – Acoustical effect achieved by placing the diaphragm of a driver element at the throat of a horn, producing a driver of greater efficiency.

HTML – (Hyper Text Markup Language) – The authoring language used to create documents on the World Wide Web.

HTTP – (Hyper Text Transfer Protocol) – The underlying protocol used by the World Wide Web. HTTP defines how messages are formatted and transmitted, and what actions Web servers and browsers should take in response to various commands. For example, when you enter a URL in your browser, this actually sends an HTTP command to the Web server directing it to fetch and transmit the requested Web page. HTTP is called a stateless protocol because each command is executed independently, without any knowledge of the commands that came before it. This is the main reason that it is difficult to implement Web sites that react intelligently to user input. This shortcoming of HTTP is being addressed in a number of new technologies, including ActiveX, Java, JavaScript and cookies. Currently, most Web browsers and servers support HTTP 1.1. One of the main features of HTTP 1.1 is that it supports persistent connections. This means that once a browser connects to a Web server, it can receive multiple files through the same connection. This should improve performance by as much as 20%.

Hub – The point on a network where many circuits are connected. Hub hardware can be either active or passive. Wiring hubs are useful for their centralized management capabilities and for their ability to isolate nodes from disruption.

HVAC – (Heating, Ventilating and Air Conditioning System) – A system that provides heating, ventilating, and/or cooling within or associated with a building.

Hybrid loudspeaker – A loudspeaker that utilizes both dynamic and planar components.

IBOC – (In Band / On Channel (digital radio))

ICSHub – ICSP Network link between ICSNet data hubs. Each hub link can operate up to 1000 feet over Category 5 wiring.

ICSNet – The Panja high–speed ICSP controlnet, it employs industry–standard Category 5 wiring and RJ–45 terminals.

ICSP – (Internet Control System Protocol) – A standard Internet protocol for system control and integration applications.

IEEE – (Institute of Electrical and Electronic Engineers) – An international professional society that issues its own standards and is a member of ANSI and ISO.

IEEE Standards – A set of network standards developed by the IEEE.

IEEE 802.1 – Standards related to network management. Refers to the broad subject of managing computer networks. There exists a wide variety of software and hardware products that help network system administrators manage a network. Network management covers a wide area, including: Security: Ensuring that the network is protected from unauthorized users. Performance: Eliminating bottlenecks in the network. Reliability: Making sure the network is available to users and responding to hardware and software malfunctions.

IEEE 802.2 – General standard for the data link layer in the OSI Reference Model. The IEEE divides this layer into two sub–layers – the data link control (DLC) layer and the media access control (MAC) layer. The MAC layer varies for different network types and is defined by standards IEEE 802.3 through IEEE 802.5.

IEEE 802.3 – Defines the MAC layer for bus networks that use CSMA/CD. This is the basis of the Ethernet standard, a network in which all nodes are connected to a single wire (the bus) that has two endpoints. Ethernet 10Base–2 and 10Base–5 networks, for example, are bus networks. Other common network types include star networks and ring networks.

IEEE 802.4 – Defines the MAC layer for bus networks that use a token–passing mechanism (token bus networks).

IEEE 802.5 – Defines the MAC layer for token–ring networks.

IEEE 802.6 – A standard for Metropolitan Area Networks (MANs).

IEEE 802.11 – A standard for Wireless LAN.

IEEE 1394 – A data communications scheme standard that manages digitization, compression and synchronization processes.

IETF – (Internet Engineering Task Force) – A large open international community of network designers, operators, vendors, and researchers concerned with the evolution of the Internet architecture and the smooth operation of the Internet. It is open to any interested individual.

IFFDL – Integrated Fiber Delivery System for voice, video and data.

ILEC's – (Incumbent Local Exchange Carriers) The regional Bell Operating Companies (RBOCs) that dominate local calling services.

Integrated Amplifier – A single unit containing both a preamplifier and a power amplifier.

Interface – (n) Something that connects two separate entities. For example, a user interface is the part of a program that connects the computer with a human operator (user). There are also interfaces to connect programs, to connect devices, and to connect programs to devices. An interface can be a program or a device, such as an electrical connector. (v) To communicate. For example, two devices that can transmit data between each other are said to interface with each other. This use of the term is scorned by language purists, because interface has historically been used as a noun.

Internet – A global network connecting millions of computers. As of 1999, the Internet has more than 200 million users worldwide, and that number is growing rapidly. More than 100 countries are linked into exchanges of data, news and opinions. Unlike online services, which are centrally controlled, the Internet is decentralized by design. Each Internet computer, called a host, is independent. The operator can choose which Internet services to use and which local services to make available to the global Internet community. Remarkably, this anarchy by design works exceedingly well. There are a variety of ways to access the Internet. Most online services, such as America Online, offer access to some Internet services. It is also possible to gain access through a commercial Internet Service Provider (ISP).

Interoperability – The easy integration of products from multiple vendors without the need for custom hardware or software.

IP – (Internet Protocol) – Specifies the format of packets, also called data grams, and the addressing scheme. Most networks combine IP with a higher–level protocol called Transport Control Protocol (TCP), which establishes a virtual connection between a destination and a source. IP by itself is something like the postal system. It allows you to address a package and drop it in the system, but there's no direct link between you and the recipient. TCP/IP, on the other hand, establishes a connection between two hosts so that they can send messages back and forth for a period of time.

IR – (Infrared) – The part of the visible spectrum that is contiguous to the red end of the visible spectrum and that comprises electromagnetic radiation of wavelengths from 0.8 to 1000 microns.

IrDA – (Infrared Data Association) – A trade association of computer and chip manufactures creating standards for high–speed communications for infrared media.

ISDN – (Integrated Services Digital Network) – An international communications standard for sending voice, video, and data over digital telephone lines or normal telephone wires. ISDN supports data transfer rates of 64 Kbps (64,000 bits per second). Most ISDN lines offered by telephone companies give you two lines at once, called B channels. You can use one line for voice and the other for data, or you can use both lines for data to give you data rates of 128 Kbps, three times the data rate provided by today's fastest modems.

ISP – (Internet Service Provider) – A company that provides access to the Internet. For a monthly and/or hourly fee, the service provider gives you a software package, username, password and access phone number. Equipped with a modem, you can then log on to the Internet and browse the World Wide Web and USENET, and send and receive e–mail. ISPs are also called IAPs (Internet Access Providers).

IXC's – (Interexchange Characters) – Commonly called long distance carriers, IXCs will continue to use SONET as all long–haul transport that must pass through two metro SONET rings, at the beginning and end of the signal transmission.

JAVA – A high–level programming language developed by Sun Microsystems. Java is an object–oriented language similar to C++, but simplified to eliminate language features that cause common programming errors. Java source code files (files with a .java extension) are compiled into a format called bytecode (files with a .class extension), which can then be executed by a Java interpreter. Compiled Java code can run on most computers. Java is a general purpose programming language with a number of features that make the language well suited for use on the World Wide Web. Small Java applications are called Java Applets and can be downloaded from a Web server and run on your computer by a Java–compatible Web browser, such as Netscape Navigator or Microsoft Internet Explorer.

Jini – (pronounced GEE–nee) – Software from Sun Microsystems that seeks to simplify the connection and sharing of devices, such as printers and disk drives, on a network. Currently adding such devices to a computer or network requires installation and boot–up, but a device that incorporates Jini will announce itself to the network, provide some details about its capabilities, and immediately become accessible to other devices on the network. Under this technology it would be possible to create distributed computing, whereby capabilities are shared among the machines on a common network. This would allow users to access the power and features of any device on the network and would free the desktop computer from holding all the memory, storage and processing power it needs for any job. For example, if a disk drive on a network had Jini capabilities, any computer on that network could use the drive as though it were its own. Because Jini has the potential to make operating systems incidental to the power of networks, some have seen Jini as an attempt to reduce the influence of Windows. The software works by passing snippets of programs, called applets, back and forth among devices. Any computer that can run Java will be able to access the code and data that passes among devices.

JPEG – (Joint Photographic Experts Group)

KH – (Kilohertz) – A term meaning 1000 cycles per second.

Kilobytes – In decimal systems, kilo stands for 1,000, but in binary systems, a kilo is 1,024 (2 to the 10th power). Technically, therefore, a kilobyte is 1,024 bytes, but it is often used loosely as a synonym for 1,000 bytes. For example, a computer that has 256K main memory can store approximately 256,000 bytes (or characters) in memory at one time. A megabyte is 2 to the 20th power (approximately 1 million) and a gigabyte is 2 to the 30th power (approximately 1 billion). In computer literature, kilobyte is usually abbreviated as K or Kb. To distinguish between a decimal K (1,000) and a binary K (1,024), the IEEE has suggested following the convention of using a small k for a decimal kilo and a capital K for a binary kilo, but this convention is by no means strictly followed.

MPOE – A Minimum Point of Entry.

LAN – (Local Area Network) – A computer network that spans a relatively small area. Most LANs are confined to a single building or group of buildings. However, one LAN can be connected to other LANs over any distance via telephone lines and radio waves. A system of LANs connected in this way is called a wide–area network (WAN). LANs are capable of transmitting data at very fast rates, much faster than data can be transmitted over a telephone line; but the distances are limited, and there is also a limit on the number of computers that can be attached to a single LAN.

LCD – (Liquid Crystal Display) – A type of display used in digital watches and many portable computers. LCD displays utilize two sheets of polarizing material with a liquid crystal solution between them. An electric current passed through the liquid causes the crystals to align so that light cannot pass through them. Each crystal, therefore, is like a shutter, either allowing light to pass through or blocking the light. Monochrome LCD images usually appear as blue or dark gray images on top of a grayish–white background. Color LCD displays use two basic techniques for producing color: Passive matrix is the less expensive of the two technologies. The other technology, called thin film transistor (TFT) or active–matrix, produces color images that are as sharp as traditional CRT displays, but the technology is expensive. Recent passive–matrix displays using new CSTN and DSTN technologies produce sharp colors rivaling active–matrix displays. Most LCD screens used in notebook computers are backlit to make them easier to read.

LCD Projection Television – Front projection television that projects liquid crystal display pixels from a single lens onto a screen.

Line Doubler – Electronic device meant to enhance a video picture by doubling the number of broadcasted lines per frame.

Line Stage Preamplifier – Stage of a preamplifier that accommodates all sources other than a turntable.

LON – (Local Operating Network) – Coined and trademarked by Echelon, a LON is the communications component in a complete network solution for control applications.

LonMark Association – The LonMark Interoperability Association design guidelines help manufacturers build interoperable LonMark products based upon LonWorks technology. Within association task groups, LonMark members develop application specific functional profiles. These profiles precisely layout the network interface for a particular controls function. Functional profiles ease the specification process and enhance interoperability without compromising the ability of specifiers to call for unique capabilities, or the ability of manufacturers to differentiate products.

MAC – (Media Access Control address) – A hardware address that uniquely identifies each node of a network. In IEEE 802 networks, the Data Link Control (DLC) layer of the OSI Reference Model is divided into two sub–layers: the Logical Link Control (LLC) layer and the Media Access Control (MAC) layer. The MAC layer interfaces directly with the network media. Consequently, each different type of network media requires a different MAC layer. On networks that do not conform to the IEEE 802 standards but do conform to the OSI Reference Model, the node address is called the Data Link Control (DLC) address.

MACRO – A lengthy series of instructions dictated to a home controller that reduces a complex process to a single command, so one button can dim the lights, lower the shades and start a movie.

Magnetic Planar Loudspeaker – Planar loudspeaker employing a large panel transducer onto which a copper wire has been attached, thus acting as a distributed voice coil across the surface.

Mbps – (megabits Per Second) – One million bits of information transference per second between two pieces of digital equipment.

MCM – (Multi–Carrier Modulation) – The principle of transmitting data by dividing the stream into several parallel bit streams, each of which has a much lower bit rate, and by using these substreams to modulate several carriers. The first systems using MCM were military HF radio links in the late 1950s and early 1960s.

Megabytes – (1) When used to describe data storage, 1,048,576 (2 to the 20th power) bytes. Megabyte is frequently abbreviated as M or MB. (2) When used to describe data transfer rates, as in MBps, it refers to one million bytes.

MHz – (megahertz) – A unit of frequency denoting one million Hertz (i.e. 1,000,000 cycles per second). Usually refers to the upper frequency band on a cabling system.

Midrange – A drive element in a loudspeaker responsible for reproducing the midband of an audible signal, typically operating anywhere between 350 Hz and 3 kHz. Also refers to those specific frequencies as well.

MMC – (Multimedia Card)

Modem – A device that converts a computer system's digital information into analog information and transmits it over a telephone line. Another modem must be used when the information is received to convert the information back from analog to digital.

MP3 – The file extension for MPEG, audio layer 3. Layer 3 is one of three coding schemes (layer 1, layer 2 and layer 3) for the compression of audio signals. Layer 3 uses perceptual audio coding and psychoacoustic compression to remove all superfluous information (more specifically, the redundant and irrelevant parts of a sound signal. The stuff the human ear doesn't hear anyway). It also adds a MDCT (Modified Discrete Cosine Transform) that implements a filter bank, increasing the frequency resolution 18 times higher than that of layer 2. The result in real terms is layer 3 shrinks the original sound data from a CD (with a *bitrate of 1411.2 kilobits per one second of stereo music) by a factor of 12 (down to 112–128kbps) without sacrificing sound quality. *Bitrate denotes the average number of bits that one second of audio data will consume. Because MP3 files are small, they can easily be transferred across the Internet. Controversy arises when copyrighted songs are sold and distributed illegally off of Web sites. On the other hand, musicians may be able to use this technology to distribute their own songs from their own Web sites to their listeners, thus eliminating the need for record companies. Costs to the consumer would decrease, and profits for the musicians would increase.

MPEG – (Motion Picture Experts Group)

MSO – (Multiple System Operator (of cable TV systems))

Multicast – An IP multicast is a mechanism for sending a single message to multiple recipients. It is useful for discovery operations where one does not know exactly who has the information one seeks.

Multicast DNS – A proposal to the IETF on rules for making normal DNS requests using multicast UDP.

NAHB – (National Association of Home Builders) – A trade association of residential builders across the United States comprised of state and local associations.

NAT – (Network Address Translation) – An Internet standard that enables a local–area network (LAN) to use one set of IP addresses for internal traffic and a second set of addresses for external traffic. A NAT box located where the LAN meets the Internet makes all necessary IP address translations. NAT serves two main purposes. It provides a type of firewall by hiding internal IP addresses and enables a company to use more internal IP addresses. Since they're used internally only, there's no possibility of conflict with IP addresses used by other companies and organizations. It allows a company to combine multiple ISDN connections into a single Internet connection.

NEC – (National Electrical Code) – A set of rules and regulations plus recommended electrical practices that are put out be the National Fire

Protection Association and generally accepted as the building wiring standard in the US.

NFBAA – The National Fire and Burglar Alarm Association.

NTSC – Video standard primarily broadcast the United States and Japan which produces 525 lines of video per frame, at a rate of 30 frames per second.

NVOD – (National Television Systems Committee)

OFDM – (Orthogonal Frequency Division Multiplexing) – A special form of MCM with densely spaced subcarriers and overlapping spectra was patented in the U.S. in 1970 OFDM abandoned the use of steep bandpass filters that completely separated the spectrum of individual subcarriers, as it was common practice in older Frequency Division Multiplex (FDMA) systems (e.g. in analogue SSB telephone trunks), in Multi–Tone telephone modems and still occurs in Frequency Division Multiple Access radio.

OSGI – The Open Services Gateway Initiative is an industry group working to define and promote an open standard for connecting the coming generation of smart consumer and small business appliances with commercial Internet services. The Open Services Gateway specification will provide a common foundation for Internet Service Providers, network operators and equipment manufacturers to deliver a wide range of e–services via gateway servers running in the home or remote office.

PAC – (Perceptual Audio Coder)

PAL – European television standard developed in Germany which broadcasts 625 lines per frame, at a rate of 25 frames per second.

PATH – (Partnership for the Advancement of Technology)

PBX – (Private Branch Exchange) – A private telephone network used within an enterprise. Users of the PBX share a certain number of outside lines for making telephone calls external to the PBX. Most medium–sized and larger companies use a PBX because it's much less expensive than connecting an external telephone line to every telephone in the organization. In addition, it's easier to call someone within a PBX because the number you need to dial is typically just 3 or 4 digits. A new variation on the PBX theme is the centrex, which is a PBX with all switching occurring at a local telephone office instead of at the company's premises.

PC–centric – Hardware, software and/or protocols dependant upon a specific PC (personal computer) to function.

Peer To Peer – A simple kind of network that sets up a conversation between two machines without a middleman (server). Both can carry out the same functions.

Planar loudspeaker – A loudspeaker that produces sound by vibrating a thin, flat transducer, commonly suspended between electrodes or magnets, in response to a signal.

Plasma Screen – A flat–screen monitor, approximately three to five inches thick, for screening digital, satellite, video, cable and television programs. It can also be used as a computer. Note: Not all plasma screens are HDTV compatible.

PLC – (Powerline Carrier) – The transmission of communication signals across utility power lines or existing home wiring. Frequencies may range from 8 kHz to 200 kHz and above. Power levels are normally in the 1 to 20 watt range. The advantages of these systems include their ability to send signals over very long transmission lines (more than 100 miles) and their reliability. However they are limited in the amount of information they can transport because of narrow bandwidths. Their low–frequency signals are severely attenuated by capacitor banks and transformers and can be overcome.

PNA – (Power Line Control)

POD – (Point of Deployment (card for open cable boxes)

Port – An entrance or exit from a network or a computer interface where a modem can be attached.

POTS – (Privately Owned Telephone Systems) – Also commonly referred to as Plain Old Telephone Service. The basic service supplying standard analog single line telephones, telephone lines and access to the public switched network.

Power Amplifier – Electronic device which increases the power of an incoming low level signal to accommodate the power requirements of a loudspeaker.

Powerline Network – A method of passing automation signals between devices connected to the electrical wiring. These signals coexist on the same wires and do not interfere with the home's power delivery. Data signals can be sent and received by X–10 or CEDus devices to turn on or off and to dim or brighten.

PPV – (Pay Per View)

Preamplifier – The control center of an audio/video system. Source component switching is done here, as well as volume and balance control. This component generally has some degree of signal amplification associated with it.

Protocol – An agreed–upon format for transmitting data between two devices. There are a variety of standard protocols from which programmers can choose. Each has particular advantages and disadvantages; for example, some are simpler than others, some are more reliable, and some are faster. From a user's point of view, the only interesting aspect about protocols is that your computer or device must support the right ones if you want to communicate with other computers.

Proximity Networking – Networks that are available to clients for the time that the clients are in a geographical area. Examples are the airport flight display, restaurant menu or shopping mall map that can be displayed automatically on a handheld device. The fundamental requirement for proximity networking is that no server–specific code need exist on the client before using the service, and no undesired code or configuration remains once service is out of range. In addition, a simple mechanism for discovering and navigating to local service is required.

PSTN – (Public Switched Telephone Network) – Refers to the international telephone system based on copper wires carrying analog voice data.

This is in contrast to newer telephone networks base on digital technologies, such as ISDN and FDDI. Telephone service carried by the PSTN is often called plain old telephone service (POTS).

PVR – (Personal Video Recorder)

QAM – (Quadrature Amplitude Modulation (for digital cable))

QoS – (Quality of Service) – A networking term that specifies a guaranteed "throughput" level (the amount of data transferred from one place to another or processed in a specified amount of time).

QSPK – (Quadrature Phase Shift Keying (for DBS))

RAM – (Random Access Memory) – A type of computer memory that can be accessed randomly; that is, any byte of memory can be accessed without touching the preceding bytes. RAM is the most common type of memory found in computers and other devices, such as printers. There are two basic types of RAM, dynamic RAM (DRAM) and static RAM (SRAM) . The two types differ in the technology they use to hold data, dynamic RAM being the more common type. Dynamic RAM needs to be refreshed thousands of times per second. Static RAM does not need to be refreshed, which makes it faster; but it is also more expensive than dynamic RAM. Both types of RAM are volatile, meaning that they lose their contents when the power is turned off.

RBOC – (Regional Bell Operating Company) – Seven ROBCs exist, each owns two or more Bell Operating Companies (BOCs). The RBOCs were carved out of the old AT&T/Bell System during the divestiture of the Bell operating companies from AT&T in 1984.

Rear Channel Loudspeaker – Loudspeaker pair which sits beside or behind the listener in a surround sound system. These speakers reproduce ambient information as well as soundtrack special effects.

Rear Projection Television – Television that forms an image by projecting a picture from behind a screen.

Receiver – A single unit containing a preamplifier, a power amplifier, and a tuner.

Residential Gateway – A device that allows consumer premise equipment connected to in-home networks to access and use services from any external network regardless of the media.

RF TECHNOLOGY – Radio frequency technology allows wireless appliances to work. In most remote controls, point-and-change infrared technology may be more common, but RF is the wave of the future. The advantage is that it doesn't have to be pointed and that its signals even penetrate walls. The disadvantage: its range is only 150 to 500 feet.

RF – (Radio Frequency) – Generally refers to data modulated over a high-frequency electromagnetic waves carrier for wireless transmission, the division of the radio spectrum from 535 kHz to 2.483 GHz.

RG6 Cable – A coaxial cable used for broadband video applications with a 20 gauge center conductor, allowing a higher bandwidth than RG59 cable. Uses standard "F" connectors for video equipment connections.

Ribbon Loudspeaker – Planar Loudspeaker with drive elements consisting of thin foil transducers placed between the pole elements of a large magnet.

RJ11 – Standard telephone jack with a four wire connection.

RJ25 – Three pair of RJ11 telephone plugs.

RJ31 – Security telephone line interconnect.

RJ45 – (Jack-45) – An eight-wire connector used commonly to connect computers onto a local-area network (LAN), especially Ethernet. RJ-45 connectors look similar to the ubiquitous RJ-11 connectors used for connecting telephone equipment, but they are somewhat wider.

ROM – (Read-Only Memory) – Computer memory on which data has been prerecorded. Once data has been written onto a ROM chip, it cannot be removed and can only be read. Unlike main memory (RAM), ROM retains its contents even when the computer is turned off. ROM is referred to as being nonvolatile, whereas RAM is volatile. Most personal computers contain a small amount of ROM that stores critical programs such as the program that boots the computer. In addition, ROMs are used extensively in calculators and peripheral devices such as laser printers, whose fonts are often stored in ROMs. A variation of a ROM is a PROM (programmable read–only memory). PROMs are manufactured as blank chips on which data can be written with a special device called a PROM programmer.

RS–232 – (Recommended Standard–232C) – A standard interface approved by the Electronic Industries Association (EIA) for connecting serial devices. Almost all modems conform to the EIA–232 standard and most personal computers have an EIA–232 port for connecting a modem or other device. In addition to modems, many display screens, mice, and serial printers are designed to connect to an EIA–232 port. In EIA–232 parlance, the device that connects to the interface is called Data Communications Equipment (DCE) and the device to which it connects (e.g., the computer) is called Data Terminal Equipment (DTE). The EIA–232 standard supports two types of connectors – a 25–pin D–type connector (DB–25) and a 9–pin D–type connector (DB–9). The type of serial communications used by PCs requires only 9 pins so either type of connector will work equally well. Although EIA–232 is still the most common standard for serial communication, the EIA has recently defined successors to EIA–232 called RS–422 and RS–423. The new standards are backward compatible so that RS–232 devices can connect to an RS–422 port.

SAF – (Spousal Acceptance Factor) – A term found most frequently on the tags used by showrooms and in esoteric stereophile magazines – as in, "the SAF on these six–foot–tall electrostatic speakers is zero." For "spouse," of course, read "wife."

Scanning Rate – Number of lines produced by a television per second, as it scans its picture onto a screen. Measured in Hz.

Script/Scripting – Another term for macro or batch file, a script is a list of commands that can be executed without user interaction. A script language is a simple programming language with which you can write scripts. Apple Computer uses the term script to refer to programs written in its HyperCard or AppleScript language.

SD – (Secure Digital (media card))

SDARS – (Satellite Digital Audio Radio Service)

SDH – (Synchronous Digital Hierarchy)

SDMI – (Secure Digital Music Initiative)

SDTV – (Standard Definition Television)

Serial Interface – An I/O (input/output) port that transmits data 1 bit at a time (in contrast to parallel transmission, which transmits multiple bits simultaneously). RS–232C is a common serial signaling protocol.

Series Wiring – A wiring method where each termination point is wired in series from the previous jack. (The same as Daisy Chain.)

Server – A computer or device on a network that manages a network's resources. For example, a file server is a computer and storage device dedicated to storing files. Any user on the network can store files on the server. A print server is a computer that manages one or more printers, and a network server is a computer that manages network traffic. A database server is a computer system that processes database queries. Servers are often dedicated, meaning that they perform no other tasks besides their server tasks. On multiprocessing operating systems, however, a single computer can execute several programs at once. A server in this case could refer to the program that is managing resources rather than the entire computer.

SGML – (Standard Generalized Markup Language) – A system for organizing and tagging elements of a document. SGML was developed and standardized by the International Organization for Standards (ISO) in 1986. SGML itself does not specify any particular formatting; rather, it specifies the rules for tagging elements. These tags can then be interpreted to format elements in different ways. SGML is used widely to manage large documents that are subject to frequent revisions and need to be printed in different formats. Because it is a large and complex system, it is not yet widely used on personal computers. However, the growth of Internet, and especially the World Wide Web, is creating renewed interest in SGML because the World Wide Web uses HTML, which is one way of defining and interpreting tags according to SGML rules.

Single Ended Amplification – Method of amplifying a signal whereby one side of the input and output amplifying devices are connected to ground.

SONET – (Synchronous Optical Network)

Spread Spectrum – A signaling technique where the AC energy transmitted by a device is spread over the range of frequencies rather than remaining concentrated at one frequency (such as an AM radio station). CEBus uses spread spectrum techniques on the power line and radio frequency devices.

SSDP – (Simple Service Discover Protocol) – The Universal Plug and Play proposal for how to perform extremely simple discovery.

Standards – Agreed principals of protocol set by committees working under various trade and international organizations.

STB – (Set Top Box) – A generic term for a device connected between the television set and the cable that performs selection and decryption processes.

Structured Wiring – A planned and organized method of residential low voltage wiring allowing for efficient hook–up and future changes and additions.

Star – A topology in which all wire drops are wired directly to a central distribution point that establishes, maintains, and breaks connection to the drops.

Subwoofer – Woofer large enough to produce frequencies from 20 or 30 Hz to 80 or 100 Hz, typically housed in its own enclosure.

Surround Sound – Attempt to recreate using more than a stereo pair of loudspeakers the acoustical and ambient information of a particular environment, such as a church, a stadium, a movie theater, etc. A surround sound decoder is a device which extracts the ambient and effects information from a recording or soundtrack and steers this signal to the appropriate amplification channels.

SWAP – (Shared Wireless Access Protocols) – Describes wireless transmission devices and protocols for interconnecting computers, peripherals and electronic appliances in a home environment.

Systems Integration – The development of a system that controls and communicates information between intelligent subsystems.

T–1 Carrier – A dedicated phone connection supporting data rates of 1.544 Mbits per second. A T–1 line actually consists of 24 individual channels, each of which supports 64Kbits per second. Each 64Kbit/second channel can be configured to carry voice or data traffic. Most telephone companies allow you to buy just some of these individual channels, known as fractional T–1 access. T–1 lines are a popular leased line option for businesses connecting to the Internet and for Internet Service Providers (ISPs) connecting to the Internet backbone. The Internet backbone itself consists of faster T–3 connections. T–1 lines are sometimes referred to as DS1 lines.

T–3 Carrier – A dedicated phone connection supporting data rates of about 43 Mbps. A T–3 line actually consists of 672 individual channels, each of which supports 64 Kbps. T–3 lines are used mainly by Internet Service Providers (ISPs) connecting to the Internet backbone and for the backbone itself. T–3 lines are sometimes referred to as DS3 lines.

TCP/IP – (Transmission Control Protocol/Internet Protocol) – A set of communications protocols to connect different types of computers over networks.

TECHHOME.ORG – (The Consumer Electronics Association's Web site) – An easy-to-follow, hype-free guide to networking a home, from the simplest systems to the most complex.

TELCO – An Americanism for a telephone company.

Telecommunications – Any transmission, emission, or reception of signs, signals, writings, images, and sounds, or information of any nature by cable, radio, visual, optical or other electromagnetic systems.

Touchcsreen – A visual display terminal screen that responds to instructions as the user touches the screen.

Transistor – A semiconductor device (usually made of silicon) used in electronic circuit. Common uses include signal amplification and voltage rectification.

Tuner – A separate AM/FM radio which is fed into a preamplifier.

Turntable – Used for the playback of long playing records, this unit rotates records at a constant speed so that an attached phono cartridge can extract a musical signal. Must be used with a tone arm and cartridge to comprise a complete playback system.

Tweeter – A drive unit in a loudspeaker responsible for reproducing the higher frequencies of an audible signal, typically active above 3 kHz.

Twisted Pair – Two insulated copper wires twisted around each other to reduce induction (thus interference) from one wire to the other. The twists, or lays, are varied in length to reduce the potential for signal interference between pairs. Several sets of twisted pair wires may be enclosed in a single cable. In cables greater than 25 pairs, the twisted pairs are grouped and bound together in a common cable sheath.

UDP – (User Datagram Protocol) – A connectionless protocol that, like TCP, runs on top of IP networks. Unlike TCP/IP, UDP/IP provides very few error recovery services, offering instead a direct way to send and receive datagrams over an IP network. It's used primarily for broadcasting messages over a network.

UI – (User Interface)

UPnP – (Universal Plug 'n Play) – An architecture for pervasive peer–to–peer network connectivity of PCs of all form factors, intelligent appliances, and wireless devices. UPnP is a distributed, open networking architecture that leverages TCP/IP and the Web to enable seamless proximity networking in addition to control and data transfer among networked devices in the home, office, and everywhere in between.

UPnP Forum – More than 60 members from different areas in the industry have joined the UPnP Forum, and 15 companies are members of the UPnP Forum Steering Committee. Initial technical working groups are Printers, Internet Gateways, Home Lighting, Home Security, Home HVAC, and Home Energy Management. The steering committee has received nominations for other working groups, especially in the AV space, and is in the process of defining and creating the new working groups.

URI – (Uniform Resource Identifier) – The generic term for all types of names and addresses that refer to objects on the World Wide Web. A URL is one kind of URI.

URL – (Uniform Resource Locator) – The global address of documents and other resources on the World Wide Web. The first part of the address indicates what protocol to use, and the second part specifies the IP address or the domain name where the resource is located.

USB – (Universal Serial Bus) – A new external bus standard that supports data transfer rates of 12 Mbps (12 million bits per second). A single USB port can be used to connect up to 127 peripheral devices, such as mice, modems, and keyboards. USB also supports Plug–and–Play installation and hot plugging. It wasn't until the release of the best-selling iMac in 1998 that USB became widespread. It is expected to completely replace serial and parallel ports.

VESA – (Video Electronics Standards Association) – A consortium of video adapter and monitor manufacturers whose goal is to standardize video protocols. VESA has developed a family of video standards that offer greater resolution and more colors than VGA. These standards are known collectively as Super VGA (SVGA).

Vacuum Tube – A multi–electrode valve that controls the flow of electrons in a vacuum from electrode to electrode. It is based on a principle known as thermionic electron emission. A common use is for signal amplification. While not often found in modern electronics, certain audio manufacturers produce high quality components utilizing these devices.

VOD – (Video on Demand)

VOIP – (sometimes called IP telephony, Voice over the Internet (VOI) or Voice over IP (VOIP) products) – A category of hardware and software that enables people to use the Internet as the transmission medium for telephone calls. For users who have free, or fixed–price Internet access, Internet telephony software essentially provides free telephone calls anywhere in the world. To date, however, Internet telephony does not offer the same quality of telephone service as direct telephone connections. There are many Internet telephony applications available. Some, like CoolTalk and NetMeeting, come bundled with popular Web browsers. Others are stand-alone products.

VPN – (Virtual Private Network) – A network that is constructed by using public wires to connect nodes. For example, there are a number of systems that enable you to create networks using the Internet as the medium for transporting data. These systems use encryption and other security mechanisms to ensure that only authorized users can access the network and that the data cannot be intercepted.

VSB – (Vestigial Sideband Modulation)

WAN – A computer network that spans a relatively large geographical area. Typically, a WAN consists of two or more local-area networks (LANs). Computers connected to a wide-area network are often connected through public networks, such as the telephone system. They can also be connected through leased lines or satellites. The largest WAN in existence is the Internet.

WAP – (Wireless Application Protocol) – Is a secure specification that allows users to access information instantly via handheld wireless devices such as mobile phones, pagers, two-way radios, smartphones and communicators. WAP is supported by all operating systems. Ones specifically engineered for handheld devices include PalmOS, EPOC, Windows CE, FLEXOS, OS/9, and JavaOS. WAPs that use displays and access the Internet run what are called "microbrowsers". These browsers have small file sizes that can accommodate the low memory constraints of handheld devices and the low-bandwidth constraints of a wireless-handheld network. Although WAP supports HTML and XML, the WML language (an XML application) is specifically devised for small screens and one-hand navigation without a keyboard. WML is scalable from two-line text displays up through graphic screens found on items such as smart phones and communicators. WAP also supports WMLScript. It is similar to JavaScript, but makes minimal demands on memory and CPU power because it does not contain many of the unnecessary functions found in other scripting languages. Because WAP is fairly new, it is not a formal standard yet. It is still an initiative that was started by Unwired Planet, Motorola, Nokia, and Ericsson.

Watt – Power specification stating the amount of energy dissipated in one second. This term is commonly associated with power amplifiers.

Wide screen – Any video software or hardware which has an aspect ratio wider than 4:3 (which is the typical television ratio). Wide screen formats are meant to reproduce the original aspect ratio of a movie as viewed in a theater.

WLAN – A wireless LAN (WLAN) is a flexible data communication system implemented as an extension to, or as an alternative for, a wired LAN within a building or campus. Using electromagnetic waves, WLANs transmit and receive data over the air, minimizing the need for wired connections. Thus, WLANs combine data connectivity with user mobility, and, through simplified configuration, enable movable LANs.

WMA – (Windows Media Audio)

WOFDM – Same as OFDM but does not rely on cable media. It is a wireless system. See OFDM.

Woofer – Drive element in a loudspeaker responsible for reproducing the lower (and sometimes midband) portion of an audio signal, ideally operating from 1 kHz down, depending on its size.

xDSL – Similar to ISDN inasmuch as both operate over existing copper telephone lines (POTS) and both require the short runs to a central telephone office (usually less than 20,000 feet). However, xDSL offers much higher speeds – up to 32 Mbps for downstream traffic, and from 32 Kbps to over 1 Mbps for upstream traffic.

XML – (eXtensible Markup Language) – A new specification being developed by the W3C. XML is a pared-down version of SGML, designed especially for Web documents. It enables designers to create their own customized tags to provide functionality not available with HTML. For example, XML supports links that point to multiple documents, as opposed to HTML links, which can reference just one destination each. Whether XML eventually supplants HTML as the standard Web formatting specification depends a lot on whether it is supported by future Web browsers. So far, the only major browser vendor to endorse XML is Microsoft, which has stated that XML will be supported in a future version of Internet Explorer.

X–10 – Home automation protocol that uses existing home wiring to broadcast a 5 volt 212kHz 1 msec (micro second) burst perfectly timed to cross the 60Hz AC power cycle. An X–10 message includes a start code, letter code and a number code.